3093527

D1409221

Lost No More...

A Mother's Spiritual Journey
Through Her Son's Addiction

Lost No More...

A Mother's Spiritual Journey
Through Her Son's Addiction

Marilyn Burns, M.S., L.P.C.C.
and
Christopher Burns

*"I guess what doesn't kill ya....
only makes you stronger."*

– Chris, August 12, 2005,
in the Collier County Jail in Florida

*"What did kill him...
has made me stronger."*

– The author,
"two years after my son's death"

To Chris, who asked me in a dream to write his story for him the night before he was taken off life support. He believed that he came to the Earth to help others and this book would be his way of fulfilling his dream, not a longer life on Earth.

Chris, this is my last labor of love for YOU. I so wish that you could write this yourself, but it is not in the divine plan. To the best of my knowledge, I have inserted every lead that you gave me to put in this manuscript for you. I hope it serves its purpose. Until we meet again, I remind myself often that you are just a heartbeat away. I pray that your spirit continues to shine brightly for all of us.

Forever in our hearts,
I love you, Chris,
Mom

DEDICATION

This book is dedicated to the lost souls who struggle everyday to find their way to a life free of drugs and alcohol. It is for Jay, Chris's brother, who made him laugh, who was his best friend and partner in crime and who brought him to one part of his "dream," which was to live in the mountains. I can remember a call from Chris somewhere in yesteryear: *"Mom, I'm sitting on the top of Mt. Tam. I have my cig and my Starbucks, my girl is sitting at my side and I'm looking at Heaven."* Thank you, Jay, for giving him a little piece of heaven during his short stay on this Earth.

It is for Stephanie, Chris's first and only love. Chris was never the same without you. You believed in him and loved him as much as any young woman could love. Thank you for loving him like you did, Steph.

It is for his childhood friends: Matt, Dave and Beaver, the four musketeers. You were partners in crime and buds till the end.

It is for his grandmother, Margie, who could never see any wrong in him. She was his number-one rescuer. She cries when she says, "He told me not to worry because he was coming back to stay with me." She believed in his words much more than he did.

It is for his high school buddies who fought for him, played hard with him, laughed with him and cried for him so deeply when he died. For those who still write to him on his MySpace page—Ryan and Billy—thank you for always being there for him. He loved you guys. Ryan, you gave him something hopeful to look forward to: a new beginning in life. Thank you for believing in him when he couldn't believe in himself.

It is for his family—his aunts, uncles, grandparents, cousins, his father Randy, stepmom Michele and stepbrother Michael. If only I could trade a second in time for every prayer, worry, loving thought and money you sent his way to help him, it would have created much more opportunity to build more memories with Chris.

It is for everyone who was touched by Chris's smile, strength, courage, charm, laughter and warmth. My hope is that you will find what you need to feel comforted when you are missing him.

It is for all of the men, women and children who tried so hard to stay close to someone they love who suffers from an addiction. You didn't fail. When you couldn't find the kind and loving words to say and didn't behave in a loving or compassionate way, these troubled souls knew that you loved them. I pray that you can love yourself as much as you love them.

It is for all of the families who have lost someone to drugs or alcohol. I hope and pray that you can find some peace.

Lastly, this is for God for bringing me to my spiritual path through my short time with Chris.

I thank all of you from the bottom of my heart for loving my son and for looking past his addiction when he needed you the most.

God Bless, Marilyn

I'm not sure where this is going or how it is going to unfold, but it is my ultimate attempt to follow the path on which my beliefs and my heart have led me. Years ago, I chose to believe that everything happens for a reason. I also chose to believe in reincarnation. I've learned to embrace the possibility that I picked the events in my life, in order to grow spiritually. I trust that someday I will understand why I could have chosen to lose a child so young in life. Perhaps by the time I write my conclusion to *Lost No More*, I will understand. My heart is telling me that writing this book is not "**my last labor of love for Chris**"; it is most likely **his labor of love for me.** As I struggle to write this book, I continue to grow. Could that be part of the divine plan? I guess I won't know until I KNOW, so until then I will trust the process.

And so this story begins, almost at the end. I can only tell you what I know and how it appeared to me. The rest is for you to figure out: why you were led to read it, and how you will allow it to work for you. If you decide to embrace the belief that you are led to the people, events and circumstances in life for your own spiritual growth, *Lost No More* will be on your gratitude list. And if you decide to embrace the belief that angels walk this Earth, you might find that Chris is one of yours. I feel strongly that the story of his life and his death will alter you in some way.

So let's walk this together. Grab your tissues and your comfort food. If you get too upset, ask Chris to help you. He is good at that. He will help you to cry, to laugh, to be one with the moment and to open your mind to new possibilities. Come with me; take a walk up to the top of Mt. Tam with Chris and to the bottom of my heart with me.

Mt. Tam in Northern California…*"It's heaven mom."*

THE END

But for me it was the beginning of the journey to the bottom of my heart....

I have been agonizing over writing this chapter. My friend Amanda suggested I write the chapters as they come to me and we put them together in the proper sequence later. I've had moments of wanting to turn back and abandon this promise to Chris but I know that I can't. He wants me to heal but I'm not sure how I can possibly do that by going through a detailed reenactment of my nightmare. What I know is this: the real nightmare of how deeply we suffered with him through his addiction is finally over. Now we can actually live life with him with some meaning and joy. We can move forward with love; the fear has finally ended. It's over now.

So here we go. *Chris, I need you more than ever now. Help me with this....*

April 18, 2007. 11:57 a.m. They say that mothers have a way of knowing when their children are in danger and I knew it was the beginning of the end when I received Jay's message that morning. I work as a counselor in my own private practice in Boardman, Ohio. It was a few minutes before I was breaking for lunch when Jay called from California, where he lived with my other son, Chris. Time stood still as I dialed the phone to call him back. I could barely understand him when we finally connected. *"Mom, Chris is not OK. You have to get here now. I don't think he's going to make it!"*

Jason explained that Chris was being taken to a trauma hospital in Novato, California. He wasn't sure what happened; all he knew was that Chris was found dead in a motel room and was resuscitated. He couldn't tell me anything more. I immediately called his father Randy. Everything moved into fast-forward at that point.

Randy had little hope and talked of making Chris's funeral arrangements, a concept that threw me into a tailspin. I had fought for years to keep Chris alive and I wasn't going to stop now. Randy and I fought many times during Chris's six-year battle with drugs. Randy believed in tough love and so do I, but I couldn't do it. Today I am glad that I didn't. Randy was right many times but this was one time when I prayed that he wasn't, and I didn't want to hear a thing he had to say about funeral arrangements. We had many calls from Chris through the years that were extremely upsetting and things always seemed to work out. This would too.

God, this is his wake up call, right? Now we will turn the bend. This is it…

Not everyone believes in angels, but as I explain in my chapter on spirituality, I became a believer twenty-four years ago when my grandmother appeared to me. I feel strongly that my angels were preparing me for my worst nightmare, Chris's death. I told several people a few weeks before he died that something was going to happen. I didn't know what; I just knew that it was going to be bad. I had a dreadful feeling that I couldn't seem to shake. My nervous system was very restless and I was preoccupied, distancing from everyone, probably getting prepared for what I knew on a soul level was next: the death of my son. Every parent who goes through this experience is fearful of that phone call, yet on some level we prepare for it. The truth is that we can never prepare for that level of trauma or loss.

Just two weeks before Jay called that morning, I woke up in a panic because I had a nightmare of Chris lying in a coffin. I was sobbing and I called him just to hear his voice. His response to the call was reassuring for me. *"Mom, what the heck? I know a lot of what you dream comes true. I promise that I will see a doctor and get some help. I promise you I will. That's scary shit, Mom. I hope it doesn't mean anything."* I prayed even harder for God to protect him and keep me strong for him. It was another surreal moment for me. The nightmare I had was my soul preparing me for what was yet to come. My soul allowed me to rehearse his funeral so I could get through it when the time came.

Randy and I couldn't get a flight out of Cleveland until 8 p.m. The flight to California was a grueling five hours. We couldn't talk to Jay when we got on the plane and couldn't get any updates until we landed in San Francisco that night. We arrived at the hospital in Novato at 3:30 in the morning. The evening guard sitting at the desk was the first to greet us. Thank God for Randy, who held himself together when I couldn't. "Up the stairs and through the doors," he said. My tears steadily flowed.

At the top of the stairs there was a room that was designated for the families of the patients. Randy and I opened the door expecting to find his sister, Judy, who had arrived earlier from Phoenix, or Jay. Instead, there was a young woman sleeping on the sofa. I recognized her. Chris couldn't wait to get to California to meet this girl. I saw her face often because soon after he fell for her, her picture became the screen saver on his computer.

She slowly sat up and apologized over and over to us. She admitted to being with Chris that night in the motel. She told us that he was complaining of not feeling well but fell asleep. She said he woke her up gasping for air. "*I propped his head back with a towel and set my alarm to check on him at six in the morning. When the alarm went off and I looked over at him, he wasn't breathing,*" she said to us.

How could you fall asleep when he couldn't breathe? Why would you leave him there and not use the phone in the room to call for help? Much of what she said made no sense to us, but they were using drugs that night and the coroner explained that he has seen many cases where drug addicts or alcoholics passed out next to the bodies of friends or loved ones. Some would even walk right over the bodies and leave the bodies to avoid the repercussions. It was way too much for my brain to wrap around; there's more on her story later. I didn't want to waste another minute; I needed to see my son.

Terror had set in as we moved through the hall to his room. It felt like I was walking through a pond of cement and I could hardly lift my leg to take the next step. It was quiet on his unit. There were only two patients on that trauma unit and one of them was Chris. The exit signs were lit and the monitor lights at the nurses' station were shadowing the hall. I was very frightened to look in his room. I could hardly catch my breath as I took my steps closer to the doorway. I took a deep breath before I made the bend into his room. His aunt Judy was sleeping on a chair propped up with some pillows. God bless her; she stayed there until the end.

This was another moment when time stood still. It was as though my eyes glanced at everything and everyone in the room but Chris. Then everything in the room disappeared. I saw my baby lying there sustained on life support, my baby boy, my beautiful Christopher. It was the quietest that Chris had been since birth. The silence in the room was deafening. The only sounds were those coming from the machines that were keeping him alive. I was waiting for him to open his eyes and talk to me. I wish I had a penny for every time he said my name. His terms of endearment were many: Mom, Ma, Madre, Marilyn, Mother, Mommy, Hey Woman and Hey Stupid (that was one of his favorites). If he were here, he would proudly add other names to the list. Ah… my baby Chris.

He was hooked up to all of the monitors or I would have crawled in bed next to him. That's all I wanted to do: rock him until he could wake up. I felt so helpless. *Chris it's me, Mom. Please just say my name. Please, Chris, just open your eyes.* Chris never said my name again. You can't imagine what that does to a mother. On Mother's Day he was the first to wake me. On Christmas he would charge into my room. *"Ma get up! Are you going to sleep all day?"* (This was how he acted as an ADULT too!) He made my birthdays fun. When he was too young to shop, his gift was a homemade coupon book. I would tear out coupons as needed, small promises he made to do the dishes, clean his room, not fight with Jay, scoop the dog poop, etc. My favorite (and of course there weren't enough of them) was "I WILL BE QUIET FOR FIVE MINUTES." My heart aches to hear his voice today. *I'm so, so sorry Chris if I ever made you feel like you were a burden to me. You never were. I just got tired at times and couldn't listen. Forgive me, Chris. I love you so much and I never meant to hurt your feelings.* As I am writing this, I know he knows that.

My relationship with him had to change, and it did. In the hospital he showed me how to have a relationship with him again. When I talk to him spiritually, I know when and how he talks back. I trust in what he tries to tell me. He is there when I need him and I KNOW that he breathes for me when I can't catch my breath from crying. *Thank you, God, for teaching me how that works.* Funny how today I can hear him clearly in the silence of my mind, usually early in the morning. I get messages from him that wake me and I write them down or record them on the recorder next to my bed so I won't forget. I trust them as much as I trust the messages I get from God. Chris tells me what he wants me to put in his book. I listen and trust that he has a reason for what he says and I don't hesitate. The information we were receiving that night from the medical team was bleak, but they told us not to give up hope. It was too soon for that. I hung onto every word, but Chris never did open his eyes or respond. Doctors had their ways to stimulate trigger points that would set off reflexes and his eyelids would open slightly. I hated when they did that. It dropped me into a deeper abyss out of which it was becoming more impossible to crawl out.

We were told to do everything and anything to try to stimulate his brain. Jay brought his favorite songs they had downloaded. We kept the headset in his ears hoping to stimulate him. The nurses said that it could be possible for the neurotransmitters to recognize a sound and create some activity in the brain. They allowed us to hold our cell phones up to his ear so we could call his friends, family and Stephanie, his true love. But nothing happened. Nothing ever happened. It was not in the divine plan I guess. Perhaps Chris was just remembering the painful memories and wanted them to finally be over.

As the days turned into nights and nights into days, what seemed like years were really just a few short days. We were getting weary and almost silly at times. My sister Cookie and her daughter Heather had arrived from Ohio. Randy and his sister Judy were there. Jay and his girlfriend Nicole left right before Chris was taken off life support and never came back to his room. I know it was too painful for Jay; almost two years later, I have a clearer understanding of what that was all about for him. Nicole was with us as much as she could be. She spent a lot of time with Chris when he lived in California. All three of them worked and lived together and grew to be good friends.

The staff encouraged us to talk to him, joke and do anything we could think of to try to stimulate his brain. So we did. We talked about old times, joking and bringing up our most favorite memories of our times with Chris. Heather shared how he got her in trouble with Grandma Margie by telling her that Heather was pregnant! Heather was the target of Chris's humor at the Sunday dinners at

Grandma Margie's. You could count on it! My mother believed every word he said. She never got to the point of knowing that she shouldn't take him all that seriously. We laughed about how he told her that his girlfriend beat him up and kicked him in the head when he was down on the ground. My mother called me in a panic. I burst out laughing. I learned quickly in life as the boys grew up that when their lips were moving, they were most likely lying! My mother never got that or just didn't want to. I'm not sure which.

Some of Chris's mullet stories came up. How could they not? I know his father is not going to like this, but many of Chris's belly laughs, and ours, came from his description of how his dad's mullets evolved through the years. Chris had an obsession with mullets. He moved to Florida for a short time, two years before he died. On his drive down south, he was passing though one of the southern states and left a message on my cell. *"Ma, even the birds have mullets down here!"*

We laughed as I told another story of his senior year in high school, when he was stopped by the police somewhere in North Lima, Ohio. They pulled him over because he didn't have a taillight. When they searched his car, they found a mullet wig in the back seat and thought that was very suspicious. To make a long story short, they impounded his car and took him to the police station. His girlfriend Steph screamed at them, saying, *"He always wears that wig!"* It didn't work. Who was going to believe that lame story? But on any given day one could find Chris driving along the road with his mullet wig flapping in the wind. Every day was Halloween for that kid! The laughter these stories conjured helped us through a difficult time, but there was still no response from Chris.... *Oh my God, we are going to lose him.* <u>I sank deeper in despair and hopelessness.</u>

Chris was not responding to any attempts to stimulate his brain and we were going to meet with the team in the morning to make some major decisions for him. The neurologists and internal medicine, urology and trauma specialists were going to take the last of the tests in the morning. We had to decide whether to take him off life support, start dialysis, start the feeding tube and other things I can't even remember now. They told us our options would be to transport him to a nursing home, which they said they'd do once they started him on dialysis and inserted a feeding tube. Many of his major organs were shutting down and we were losing all hope that he was going to recover from the lack of oxygen to his brain. I saw people's lips moving but could not hear their words because I was talking to God and Chris and that was all I could do at times. I missed things that were being said, Judy, Cookie and Randy filled me in as best they could. Strangely enough, I was beginning to form my relationship with Chris as I know it today. There were times when I questioned whether the physicians, nurses, priests and nuns actually said something to me or if my angels whispered those things in my ears, as I needed to hear them. I guess it doesn't matter now.

I needed to sleep but was afraid of missing that sacred moment when my son might open his eyes. I prayed so hard that Chris would be okay and that he could eventually take over my counseling practice and live the life of which he had spoken many times through the years. I felt that my son was not ready to die and was dedicated to fighting his demons and helping others to overcome theirs. I believed in him and I believed in what he told me because I wanted it to be the truth.

When I had a moment, I sent an email to my Cursillo contact so the Christian community of which I was a part could put him on a prayer list. Everyone who knew of the situation was praying for us. My office staff and peers at my Treat Yourself Center for Holistic Health were praying and calling me on speakerphone to get updates. Family and friends were on standby waiting to hear some good news. It was a tender time in my life. To know that so many people loved us and prayed for us was the silver lining in the experience.

I sent this note via email on 4/22/07 at 11:53 p.m. from my son's computer to my friend Nancy who then forwarded it to the prayer chain in the Cursillo community in the Catholic Church.

"My Dear Brothers and Sisters in Christ,
There is but one piece of mail for the prayer chain
tonight. As you read it, you will see why. It is writ-
ten to all of us. I think of today's Gospel, 'Do
you really love me???' This mother has said with the
heaviest of hearts, Yes…..
Please pray with me."(Written by Nancy)

> *"To my Cursillo family,*
> *I am sitting here with a very heavy heart. I*
> *know that today will be the day that they will*
> *recommend that I take my son off life support.*
> *But as you know, he is my baby. I started out*
> *feeling the unfairness of it all because I have*
> *to do such an unbelievable thing. But, I know*
> *that God has blessed me that I am here today*
> *ready to reach deep into my soul to understand*
> *my relationship with Him. It is ONLY through Him*
> *that I can find a moment of peace. I don't know*
> *how to be a mother without my two sons. I raised*
> *them alone since they were four and six when*
> *their father left. My Christopher has been sent*
> *to me as an angel. He is already working mira-*
> *cles for all of us. I am reaching for anything*
> *I can, to find my courage, faith and strength to*
> *do what I need to do for him. I asked Him for*
> *a miracle….ANYTHING that might help me to know*
> *where to go next…and what I got was this…Chris*
> *has both lungs punctured and several ribs bro-*
> *ken, yesterday he got pneumonia, his intestines,*
> *bowel, kidneys have shut down, the cortex part*

of the brain is dead which is the human part. If we keep him alive, he will never walk or talk again…he will remain in a vegetative state. He started having convulsions last night. I know as his mother that I have to love him enough to let him go. I have taken such good care of him throughout his life and now will be the final opportunity for me to show him how much I love him…as I let him go. He is my greatest teacher in life. God blessed me with Chris to find my way to Him. Pray for all of the families that are suffering from addiction. But I KNOW that God has blessed them also with a way to find their faith, hope and belief in Him. My thanks to my Cursillo family…God has given us our Earth families to support one another and I can't be more thankful to all of you. I felt some peace in some strange way through this. I know God is working overtime for all of us. When a mother loses a child…all the mothers of the world weep. God is with us all right now. Marilyn Burns #55"

Nancy's beautiful prayer response that was sent to the prayer list was as follows:

"Lord, what can I say? We are mothers, fathers, sons, daughters, brothers and sisters, Lord, the pain of it all. We know Chris was not rational, he was ill. He suffered in his illness, in his addiction. Now he has left and we must believe he is with you, healed completely and wholly. His mind is clear and now he knows the power of the prayers that came to you before him. With heavy hearts, for the loss, we try to thank you. To thank you for taking him from something he

could not leave on his own. We say, eternal rest grant unto him, O Lord, and my perpetual light shine upon him. May his soul and souls of all the faithfully departed, rest in peace. Amen.

We ask you to hold Marilyn in your loving hands. Embrace her, Lord. Love her even more. Give her that peace that can only come from you. You are the Divine Healer. Take this woman's wounded heart and hold it and comfort it and help her to believe that her life is NOT over; she still has another son, who grieves his brother and loves his mother. And yes Lord, ever since your mother wept for you, the world weeps with each mother at the loss of a child. And the fathers, they weep also...as do the brothers and sisters. Lord, we love you and we cry out to you and we pray in your name, as you have told us. We thank you for the lessons learned from this experience... Hear us O Lord. Amen.

Chris and Nicole worked at the Outback restaurant in California and the owner brought hot food to us every day that we were there. He also worked for a local pizzeria at the end of his street and the owner gave us pizzas, bread, etc. to keep us as nourished as possible. Everyone was magnificent. We had healthy food to sustain us when we could and felt like eating. The off duty nursing staff called from home wanting updates on his progress. As the time was getting closer, the energy was building for him to go on his way, to whatever was next for him. *Thank you everyone for being there. You were the light that shone brightly for us when ours faded.*

However, decisions had to be made. The hospital couldn't house someone who would be sustained on life support. The team met with us and told us that they were willing to run one more brain wave test in the morning; if it continued to show no activity, there was no hope. He would be transported to a nursing home where he could live for years on dialysis and tube feedings. He would never be able to walk or talk. He would only be able to respond when his reflexes were stimulated, and that was just a knee-jerk response.

Randy and I were in conflict over the decision. He felt that Chris needed to be let go because he wouldn't want to live like that. As his mother, I felt that he didn't want to go because the

> Chris please give us strength today and tomorrow as we say goodbye to you… help us to find an understanding in this tragedy and reassure us that you are alright. (www.myspace.com/burnz2)

paramedics had revived his heart twice after he died. They worked on him to the point that both lungs were punctured, he had eight broken ribs, pneumonia had set in, his lungs had collapsed and he was still with us. He was trying to tell us that he wanted to be here.

I went to a quiet place to be alone and after praying and thinking everything through as well as I could, I decided that I wanted to give Chris my brain if that was possible. I didn't know if it could be done medically. I made up my mind that I wanted to die in order for Chris to live. I didn't tell anyone of my decision because I knew how upsetting it would be for Jay, but I felt that he would eventually be happy if he had his brother back in his life. My simple mind said that if Chris had my brain, he wouldn't be an addict and would grow old with Jay, God willing.

When I was able to talk to the neurologist alone, he said that it wasn't possible to give him a brain transplant. He said that we haven't gotten that far yet even in the studies with animals. There are too many nerve endings in the brain to transplant it. I started to sob and he grabbed my hand and looked me in the eyes and said, *"Marilyn, there are things worse than death, and keeping Chris on life support would be one of those things."*

I tried to wrap my heart around that statement for comfort's sake, but I was still in major conflict. And then, I was knocked off my axis again. All I know is that night, the night before he was taken off life support, I lay down on a couch with a pillow and blanket. My sister was on the sofa right next to me. I looked over at her to make sure she was there. I thought, *God is giving me a moment's peace.* My eyes were swollen from crying and my heart was so heavy with grief. There was a dim light in the room and the temperature was comforting, a bit cool to the touch. My body temperature was higher than normal. I moved from being chilled to sweating. I just couldn't get comfortable. But for a moment, I found some comfort and looked over at my sister and then I drifted off.

My son came to me. We talked about his death. He said that he needed me to let him go. He said he had already left his body. He apologized for creating so much pain for us; he just wanted us to be happy because he loved us so much. He told me I was the best mom that he could have ever had. He said that he came to the Earth to help others just like we talked about many times before. But he wanted me to try to accept that his way of helping others was not as we planned. He said that it would be through a book that he asked me to write for him. *"Promise me you will write this book for me, Ma. It is the only way that I can do what I came to do. It's not going to be a longer life on Earth."* I clearly remember being mad at him; I called him lazy and said he needed to write his own book. *Get back here and do it yourself! It's just like you to expect me to do the hard stuff!* We were actually laughing in the dream. Tearfully, he repeated himself, hugged me, thanked me, told me he loved me very much and he was gone.

Did Chris answer my prayers? I'll never know, but like many times since his death and during my years with him, I have grown into a true believer. I choose to believe in his final words and how they came to me. *"Mom, you have to let me go. I'm already gone."* I knew what I had to do for him. I shared my dream with everyone who would listen. I walked into his room feeling lighter, feeling like I could do what he asked me to do because that was my claim to fame as a mother. I could never say no to my boys and still can't. I am addicted to making them happy. Because Chris asked this of me, I knew I could do it. *Thank you, little love. I'm not sure if I could have let you go for any other reason other than you asked.*

Randy and I agreed that it was time. The results showed seizure activity only. He started having convulsions. The medication was keeping his body alive and nothing more would come of that. Chris' kidneys shut down through the night and he was very toxic. His body was hard by morning and swollen. I knew in my heart that he couldn't pull out of this and I also knew that he wouldn't want to live this way. His life as he knew it was over. I had to give him my last gift and that was to let him go. He couldn't do it on his own and that was why he asked me to do it for him.

When I held his hand in the hospital bed and stroked his forehead, I remembered when he was much younger and how firmly he held my hand when he was frightened. I prayed that he would make the slightest movement, but there was nothing. "He is gone now," said the nun who was sent in to console us. She squeezed my hand and, for a millisecond, I felt an adrenaline surge until I realized that it wasn't Chris's hand, it was hers. I found myself holding someone else's hand as tightly as he has held mine at times, I had to learn to begin my life without him. His words played on my mind. *"Don't worry, Ma. I know what I'm doing."*

…your memory and legacy as Chris Burnz will go on forever in my heart and in the hearts of others. (www.myspace.com/burnz2)

The staff assured us that they would keep him comfortable once they removed the life support. They said it would take about twenty minutes or so for him to go. We made the decision for them to put him on morphine for the pain and Xanax to keep him comfortable. We could stay in the room if we wanted to. Randy did, but I had to step on the other side of the curtain. I told him that I would breathe for him until the end. I had lost my mind by this point and believed that I could do that for him. I was traumatized when I heard the noise as he struggled to breathe on his own. His breathing was loud and very labored. I will never in my lifetime forget the strength in his voice. I kept on saying over and over in my mind, *"It's almost over little love. You can do it. Let me breathe for you. You are my hero Chris. Let go, love, and find Grandpa. Let him help you, grab his hand, honey. I can't give you mine anymore. I'm so sorry Chris. I can't give you mine anymore.* All I could say over and over to him was how sorry I was that I couldn't help him anymore. I felt like I failed; I couldn't keep my child alive. I was so lost and didn't know where to go.

As strong and grounded as I am in my beliefs, I floated down to a place where I've never been before. That place now has a name: the **bottom of my heart**. I have floated down there a few times since. I would like to take a minute to tell you about it. No one can go there with me, but when I arrive, my God awaits me there. It is a similar experience to the one I had with my grandmother. He talks to me and I know He is there but I can't see Him or touch Him. I feel Him though. When I arrive He lets me rest. I tell Him *I can't do this anymore* and He quietly sits and lovingly listens to me. He always reminds me of what I came here for and He tells me that if I want to continue, I can. I have to decide. Once I do, it seems as though He blows oxygen back into my lungs, opens my ears to the sounds of nature and music, opens my eyes to colors and helps me to feel how comforting my pillow is against my head at night and how laughter feels to my internal organs. He kisses me on my forehead and tells me that He is always there for me, that I am never alone. My God is an awesome God. I once mentioned to a woman I know that I wonder what He looks like and she said for me to look in the mirror and I will find Him there. I will never forget those words.

What should have taken twenty minutes took twelve hours. I felt very conflicted by the sixth or seventh hour. I began to panic because I thought we had made a mistake. He must have wanted to live because he was fighting so hard. The Catholic priest and nun prayed with us and assured us that we were doing the right thing. They said that he was probably above his body looking down on us. I realized that was true when Chris made me want to laugh in the midst of that horrible trauma.

My sister, Cookie and I were distracted by the very strong fragrance of the nun's perfume. The perfume was so strong that I could hardly breathe! I looked over at Cookie who was standing across the bed from me. I could tell she wanted to laugh. She later commented that the nun must have purchased it at the Dollar General store! I can't remember her name, but I do remember that, she hung onto me for dear life. She was holding me up, just like how I picture the Footsteps poem. I leaned into her and she totally supported my tired and frightened body. But her perfume was actually making me nauseas and I could hear Chris's belly laugh in my mind. It was so comforting for me to be so aware of his presence. He loved to belly laugh and he was entertained by my thoughts that I couldn't breathe. He laughed hard like he did many times when he saw me trip or spill something on myself.

Here is another interesting piece to the story about the Catholic nun. She gave my sister and me her card and asked us to contact her if we ever needed to talk. I wanted to do that after the dust settled. I wanted her to know how much I appreciated all that she did for me (and to send her a bottle of Angel perfume by Thierry Mugler.) I was hoping that she might like the perfume and perhaps I'd be helping others that can't breathe around her! It is my favorite and how appropriate is the name?? Shame on me! However, neither one of us could find her card. I called the hospital to get some information on her, and they didn't know about whom I was talking. She had the most piercing blue eyes;

when I looked into them, I felt like I could see into her soul. I'm choosing to believe that she was an angel that helped me to learn quickly how I was never going to lose Chris... he would always be there when I needed him. *Thank you God for sending her to me.*

Chris also made us laugh when we were in the fourth or fifth hour. It dawned on me that he was getting morphine and Xanax. *Chris, you probably think you died and went to heaven, but you didn't... You have to let go!* I was concerned that he would think he WAS in heaven on that combination of drugs. During times like that, it was so confusing. I wanted him to LIVE but by then, I wanted him to let go, as it was unbearable to watch him suffer. I will be eternally grateful that he could help us laugh a little. He still continues to help us in his own way.

Thank you, little love.

By the tenth or eleventh hour, my sister and I were totally exhausted and decided to rest for a few minutes. Judy and Randy were going to stay in the room and would let us know as he got closer to the end. They fell asleep and that was when Chris peacefully left. Judy came to get us. *"Mar, you guys better get in here,"* she said.

I was paralyzed with fear. The dreaded moment was here. The walk across the hall was a walk in time like no other. The past, present and future flashed before me. I was in a space all alone. I opened the doors and all I heard was silence. He was gone. The hope that I had hung onto for years was gone. I would never know what his children would look like, would never get to see his face when he graduated from college, would never get to watch him blow out birthday candles and would never get to grow old with him. I didn't want to walk into that room. I wanted God to take me with him instead. I couldn't breathe; all I was getting was, *take my hand, Mom. I can help you now.*

I somehow found the courage to walk in his room and when I looked at him; his face touched me so deeply. He looked like he did when he was little once he fell asleep. His head was resting on his left shoulder. All I could see were his long beautiful eyelashes and the peace in his face. I still long to find that peace. The long and hard battle was over for him. There was nothing left to say; there was nothing left to do. I was one in the moment for the first time in my life. He left me knowing how that feels.

I was aware of the energy in the room. It was lighter. The sun was rising and there was a glow from the only window that faced his bed. I was fully aware that his soul had left his body. His spirit was gone. It felt like a light spring shower cleansed the room. A new day had begun. There was a strong sense of peacefulness and serenity. My son was free. *Thank you, God, for allowing me to see the beauty in that moment. It was magnificent.*

SPIRITUALITY – OUR TEACHERS

I was born and raised Catholic. I'm grateful for my Catholic upbringing because it left me with my concept of the higher power, which I call God. My spiritual beliefs have led me to my understanding of how God works in my life and that everything happens for a reason. As a result,

> Chris I can't believe this has happened… you are the one person who has touched so many lives. Thank you for all of the great memories…
> (www.myspace.com/burnz2)

I believe that we have very important decisions to make in life. God gives us free will, which leaves us with a huge responsibility. Deciding what to believe and how to behave are such wonderful freedoms, but those freedoms come with consequences that many of us are fearful of facing. When we don't exercise our free will, we cannot blame others for how our life unfolds.

I have also chosen to believe in angels, and that they do exist on this Earth. Most people in general have accepted the concept that angels exist in the spirit world. But I believe that we have people who walk the Earth who are also interested in helping us to be better people and to live happy and meaningful lives: our Earth angels.

Many years ago, before Randy and I had Chris and Jay, I was very curious about the spiritual world. Before Jay was born, I had an interesting life-altering experience after my paternal grandmother passed away. Her name was Bertha and we were very close. She was born in Italy and came to the United States with my father when he was around two years old. She had fourteen children, five of whom passed away early in life. My father was the oldest of the nine children who survived.

One thing that sticks out as I remember my grandmother is that she was a devout Catholic woman. She prayed the rosary daily. She carried them around and she could be heard mumbling the Our Father and Hail Mary's under her breath. From watching my grandmother pray, I came to believe that prayer was special and it was the way to communicate to those in spirit form, like God. Because I loved and trusted my grandmother unconditionally, I never doubted her wisdom.

In 1980 my grandmother was diagnosed with kidney failure. She suffered for months. She was in treatment with several physicians at the time and seemed to be responding, but I knew deep in my heart that I had to prepare myself for her death. During this time, Randy and I had a long weekend trip planned. I had a long talk with her and she assured me that she was going to be fine and it was a good time for us to go away. I really didn't believe that she was that close to death, or I would not have left.

We didn't have cell phones then, and I didn't have the foresight to leave the hotel name and number with my parents when we left. (Obviously, I didn't worry a lot back then.) The night that my grandmother died, I woke up suddenly from my sleep, panicked and unable to catch my breath. I couldn't understand what was wrong, but I eventually fell back to sleep. The next morning Randy and I were driving home from our weekend and stopped by to see my parents on the way home.

No one was there, which I thought was odd, and when we walked into their kitchen; my grandmother's obituary was cut out of the paper and lying on the kitchen table. As you can imagine, it was a horrific shock for me. The days were a blur as I went through the process of her funeral.

Several months after my grandmother passed, I was going upstairs to bed. When I entered the hallway, and looked into the bedroom where we put my grandmother's bedroom suite after her death, she was sitting on the end of the bed, smiling at me. She had on a red robe that I had bought for her, one that she often wore. I was so frightened; I didn't know what to do. I ran back down the steps panicked and sobbing. Randy thought I had lost my mind—and of course I did too!

I calmed down as much as I could and we both walked up the stairs together in anticipation. I was so relieved when she wasn't there. I had been grieving so heavily over her death that I just assumed it was my mind playing tricks on me.

Today I would most likely have a different reaction to that event. However, I had no concept of spirituality and life after death and I simply reacted as though I had seen a ghost! I was afraid to tell anyone what had happened since Randy did not see my grandmother. I was a trained therapist. I assumed that I was seeing things and so I knew to not let anyone know. Eventually I got up the nerve to tell my parents and I was surprised at their reaction. My mother called a priest and explained what had happened. He assured her that there was nothing to fear, and if my grandmother ever appeared again to ask her what her purpose was in appearing, that she had come to tell me something that I needed to know and to not be frightened but trust her. The ONLY reassuring thing was that I wasn't the ONLY one who had lost their mind; the priest was as crazy as me!

This was many years ago, and you can imagine how frightening this experience was for everyone who knew of it. I prayed that she wouldn't appear again. Several weeks passed, and I was much calmer. I was able to go upstairs without hesitation. During this process, I kept the bedroom door closed and didn't go in "her" room since I had no reason to do so. But as time passed, I wanted to get on with things so I left the bedroom door open. The bedroom suite reminded me so much of her, and I was beginning to feel silly making such a big thing out of what I concluded was nothing. But one night, several months later, my grandmother reappeared in that same position with that same red robe on. She sat there motionless once again, smiling.

She has something to say; don't be frightened of her. I slowly walked into the room, and sat down on the bed next to her. It was a strange thing, but when I sat down, I couldn't see her anymore but I knew she was there. I couldn't hear her words but knew what she was saying. She wanted me to know that she was happy and that she was with my grandpa. She loved me and that I needed to get on with my life. She was in a better place and out of pain. I could feel her because she held my hand. My years with my grandma had taught me to trust her. I sat there alone, crying, and she left after she told me what she had come to say. I asked her to please come back and sit with me longer. But she was gone, and I never did see her again. Had I lost my mind, or did she lovingly lead me to my spiritual path? Little did I know how much that event would prepare me for my son's death.

I eventually came to terms with my grandma's death; her appearance prepared me for my spiritual journey. Since that event, I chose to believe that life exists after death and the soul goes on to experience other things. About three years later, I was sitting in Arthur Treacher's eating with Randy and I felt my grandmother put her hand on mine. She held it long enough for me to know that she was there. My eyes filled with tears and I told Randy that she was there. A second later, she was gone; to my knowledge she never tried to contact me again. I cry just thinking about what a loving thing she did for me. Those experiences have helped me with my son's death and other difficult passages in life.

I feel strongly that my grandmother was my first spiritual teacher on this Earth. She paved the way for the other losses that I have experienced in my life. I know that life exists in some form after death.

My sons and I have shared with one another what we believe happens after death. I doubt that I'm any different from other moms when I say that I've often wondered if they listened when I spoke. I learned after my father's sudden death in 2000 that Chris really paid attention to the things that we talked about. He not only understood but he applied his beliefs and they worked for him. I'm not as sure about Jay because he is much less verbal about his beliefs. He might not have formulated them yet or he just isn't as open in sharing them. Perhaps someday I'll know him as well as I got to know Chris.

My dad died January 1, 2000 from congestive heart failure. The boys idealized my father. Being the patriarch in our one-hundred-percent Italian family made him a BIG SHOT with my sons. There isn't enough time for me to write down the many stories he made up about his life to make it even more intriguing for the boys. They wanted to be in the Mafia. Chris's idol as a young boy was Sylvester Stallone. Who knows what story my dad told him about Sylvester. As adults, Jay and Chris had posters of Marlon Brando, Al Pacino, Stallone and scenes from *The Godfather* on their walls. In fact, when Chris was on life support, the medical staff suggested that we put on his favorite movie and keep it playing in the background to try to stimulate his brain, so my niece Heather found *The Godfather* on TV.

Sundays were always spent at my parents for dinner. My dad sat at the head of the dinner table and all of his grandchildren sat around him listening to the *creative* ways he talked about his experiences in life. My sons definitely followed in their grandpa's footsteps.

My dad was always at Jay and Chris's football practices and never missed any of their games. He took the time to have a pretty consistent relationship with my sons and I was very grateful for that. He had a heart attack in his sleep and my sister Bonnie found him dead on New Year's Day in 2000. His death was very difficult for everyone who knew him and loved him. He can never be replaced in the hearts of his family and friends. He was the heartbeat of our family and we realized that after he passed.

A few days after my father died, Chris was sitting with me at the kitchen table and as I was sobbing he said, "*Mom, remember all the times you said that everything happens for a reason? Well, I think that Grandpa needed to go for some reason, and now we have an awesome guardian angel to look over us.*" Chris really got my attention when he said those words. And of course, I was so amazed that he really did decide to adopt a belief system that was working for him. I knew that it would help him to get through difficult times. Little did I know that it would help me through his addiction and his death. When I went through his room after he passed away, I found a paper that he wrote which explains it clearly.

Chris Burns

This year can be summed up as kind of a live, learn and move on kinda year. It started off the brand new year as a drastic and horrid thing which happened to me and my family. The leader of the family, the one in the family who made everyone laugh, always smiled, always helped out, especially was always there for anyone, and was very special and meant a lot to everyone died. My grandpa died on New Years day of 2000, and it was the worst thing I ever had to go through. The call was around 8 in the morning, and not only was I extremely hung over, but I was sick as well. My mom called over my friends house which I was staying at and woke me up to hear... "grandpas dead, grandpas'dead. It was hell, I completely went into shock and everything was slow motion from there. The drive home was so horrible. Once I went to his house there was a priest praying over him and I couldn't take it. I had to leave and go home and I just sat in my room staring and thinking for like 2 days, then I finally realized that everything happens for a reason, and death is inevitable, no one can stop it, and when it's time to go, it's time to go. I was able to get through my grandpas' death after the funeral and everything. I learned a lot from this experience. I learned that no one can stop death, what happens in life happens for a reason and no matter what happens one must move on from it and not grieve forever. All that can be done after a loved one is gone, is remember all the times that were shared, and just move on from it.

After this incident occurred, I almost died by getting nailed and totaled my car. I was thinking that this was going to be the worst year ever. Then after that incident, their was a clearing. I found a perfect girl for me who is nice, smart, beautiful, pleasant and everything I need in a girl. She's cool and I really like her a lot. After I met her it seems everything good happened. I pulled up my grades, I started lifting and got my size back, I got a job, and I'm just living life to the fullest. Some things happen in life that are unexpected and catch one off guard, but what ever happens just live, learn, and move on.

(a typewritten copy of this letter can be found in the Index page 120)

It was about a week after my father died and I was sitting at a computer trying to get some work done and the printer came on by itself. A sheet of paper came out of the printer tray. Without thinking, I loaded it back. Later when I printed out the letters that I was working on that day, I saw a very small heart in the upper left hand corner of the page. I knew it was my father and I showed my children who are also believers. I'm sharing this with you because it is significant.

Three years ago, Chris was sitting at the computer and the printer came on and the same thing happened, the same exact heart was printed in the same corner of the paper. We both knew that my father wanted us to know that he was around and that he loved us.

After Chris passed away, Jay had the same experience. This past Christmas, he mentioned that he didn't feel Chris around him anymore. That night, when he was at the computer, the printer came on, and the blank sheet with the heart in the upper left hand corner came out of the tray: Chris was trying to tell him that he was wrong and he loved him very much.

I feel that it is important to decide if and how a loved one can be communicating to us. It helps to bridge the gap with the spirit world and ease our grief. Chris has done some really awesome things to con-

> Chris, last night I had a dream that me and you were hanging out in my living room like we did so many times. I didn't even know if it was a dream bc it was so real. (www.myspace.com/burnz2)

vince me that he is around. Twice, he turned on an angel lamp in the middle of the night. It is a fiber-optic lamp that changes colors when it is on. You have to pick it up and turn the small switch to the on position before it activates. I wish I could see him lift that up and turn it on. He does manage to drop it so I wake up and see the angel lit up in my room. It's so comforting to me. I know how my children must have felt when I tucked them in at night and kissed them on their cheek. I feel much love from him when I know he is in the room somewhere close by. The beauty in that is in knowing that it is a choice on my part that really brings me comfort. None of us can ever know what's really going on, but choosing to believe that something loving is occurring is very wise. What I love most about doing so is that no one can take that away from me.

If you have sons you can understand why you can have ongoing arguments about the toilet seats! Chris had a habit of lifting the lid on the seat and in the middle of the night when I needed to use the toilet, I'd be alarmed when I collapsed into the bowl. Why I was surprised every time it happened, I still don't know. I can't tell you how often we argued about the toilet seat! There have been a couple of mornings since his death that I woke to find the toilet seat up in both bathrooms. I live alone, and I know it isn't me! In fact it happened twice in the two weeks before this writing. I now use it as a check and balance system. When something happens around the house that might be Chris communicating, I check to see if the toilet seat is up or down.

He does so many things characteristic of when he was alive. It makes me wonder what he is like now. I wonder if he still looks the same and talks the same. He gives me evidence with funny or cute things that that lead me to believe that he is the same guy that he was when he died two years ago. I hope I know him when I cross over. I have fantasies that he will pick me up and twirl me around like he did when he was playful or showing off to his girlfriends!

Jay told me that right before Chris died he repeatedly played the song "How to Save a Life" by The Fray. The first Christmas after Chris passed away, it was very difficult to decorate the Christmas tree and hang the stockings. It was heart-wrenching to see the homemade ornaments that my boys had made me through the years. I had so many beautiful holidays with them. That was another moment when I felt the pain clear in the bottom of my heart. I sobbed so hard I couldn't catch my breath. Just then, "How to Save a Life" came on the stereo, and I felt Chris around me. It helped to know that he was there. I even felt his sorrow for me. I know he is deeply sorry for the pain that we go through and I pray that he has an understanding of why this was necessary and is consoled by that. He endured enough pain on the Earth and I pray he is free of it now.

Many of his friends and our family have given very clear examples of Chris's communications with them. There is no doubt in my mind that he is here with us when we need him. One of our neighbors who grew up with him said that a few months after he passed away, Chris appeared to him. He said that he went out to take a smoke break at work and when he walked outside, Chris was standing there with a very serious look on his face. He was very frightened and ran back inside. Later that night, one of their friends overdosed on drugs, and when he was told the story about Chris, it helped him to make his decision to go into treatment. I guess we will never know how to wrap our brains around these events but this young man found a beautiful way of allowing it to change the course of his future. Knowing Chris, that is exactly what he wanted to do for his friend who was in need.

About a month ago, I decided to sell the futon that was once in his room. It was the last thing that he slept on before he moved back to California. I sold the futon on a Thursday evening. A few days later I get an email from a friend of mine, Patricia. She said, "I've had dreams of Chris for the past three days now. The last one was about the pipes in your house. Leaking all through the house… maybe older pipes." (The day before, Jay's pipes started to leak all over his kitchen.) "He was laughing and smiling 'cause while you were looking at the pipes, he took your mattress 'cause he was upset he didn't have one." I couldn't even believe it. I just LOVE when he lets me know that he is around. I told my sister I started thinking that I should set up another bed because he just might be sleeping here at night. What a comforting thought.

In 1996 when we moved in the house I own today, Chris wanted the glow-in-the-dark stars all over his ceiling. He had so many of them that it really did look like he was sleeping under the stars. This past August, I heard his bedroom floor creaking. This happens a lot when he wants me to know he is in his room. I smiled because he wasn't knocking it off and I assumed he was trying to annoy me, like he often did. After a few minutes of this, I got up just to see if there was another explanation for the creaking floor. When I walked into the room, the entire ceiling was lit like I'd NEVER seen it before. The stars were so bright and they haven't glowed in several years because they are so old. He made me cry that night. I knew he was standing somewhere near me, smiling and most likely hugging me.

Ever since Classmates.com was founded, I have gotten emails about friends who signed my guestbook and left messages. I haven't been on there for years. Last year I was being led to go into the site. The Classmates.com window kept popping up and finally my intuition and curiosity was strong enough that I opened the site. When I looked at the friends who have attempted to communicate with me, there he was, Chris Burns, 2002 graduate of Boardman High School. He was on my guestbook in January 2007 just a few months before he died. Since I didn't open the site, I never accepted him as a friend and can never know now what was written. He had me crying that night too.

Every Christmas Stephanie, Chris's high school sweetheart, comes to visit Jay and me and we share many stories and laughs about Chris. This past year we were sitting at my kitchen table and suddenly the large-screen TV went on in the family room. We knew it was Chris for two reasons. One was that you must hit four buttons on three different remotes to turn on the TV, cable box and DVD player to even watch something. No surprise that the person who designed the system has some ADHD going on between their ears! The other is that the program that was on was *Intervention*, a show on A&E about addiction. Ever since Chris began to struggle with opiates, we started watching that program every Sunday night. We would remind one another at 10 that it was starting. We were so excited because we knew he wanted us to know that he was there with us, like old times! It was so sweet of him to do that. *Thank you, sweetie, for showing us that you were there.*

I've also heard several stories from Stephanie about being contacted by Chris. She told me that after he died the water in the kitchen sink would turn on sporadically. This was his clear message to her that he was there with her. She spoke of walking across campus on a day when there was a heavy downpour. It was a really bad day for her and she couldn't stop crying. She recalls feeling his arm around her as though he was holding an umbrella for her. She said that it dawned on her when she walked into a building on campus that she didn't have an umbrella and she wasn't wet!

One of his childhood buddies told me that he had a dream about Chris a few weeks after he died. Chris appeared to him and he really felt it was real. He looked at Chris in shock and said, "*I thought you were dead!*" Chris confirmed that he had died but came to say good-bye.

After Chris passed, Jay wanted a photo of his brother's hands because he intended to have a tattoo placed on his heart as a dedication to his life with Chris. The nurses placed Chris's hands in the prayer pose and a photo was taken. A few weeks after his funeral, Jay took the picture of Chris's hands to tattoo artist Debbie Lenz at Artistic Dermagraphics in our hometown. He wanted that photo on his heart with the script "Until We Meet Again." Just as Debbie was finishing the outline, Jason lamented on the fact that he didn't feel Chris's presence. In that moment, Jason shared with me that the power went out in the tattoo salon and Debbie told him that it never happened in all of their years there.

I'm sure there are many more stories to share with you. Each is significant in its own way. They are significant for the non-believers because you have to decide what to do with these facts. Do you dismiss them or try to open your mind to the possibility that the soul lives on? For the believers, these are more of an opportunity to develop stronger intuition and trust. There were many times when I would dismiss strange things by saying, "O*h that was just a noise or it was just the wind, or I was dreaming.*" I was always looking for other explanations, but I no longer do that. I've surrendered to the belief that Chris is here at times and when he is, he attempts to let me know. It is a real challenge to wrap your *brain* around it, but it takes moments to wrap your *heart* around it. It is comforting to know that our departed loved ones are here with us when they can be.

ME I AM SPECIAL

It seems like the beginning was so long ago. Some parts I don't remember as clearly as I should but I guess most of us experience that with age. I had a mammogram done last year and the tech asked me a question about my health and I couldn't remember the answer. I made a joke out of it. I suggested she ask me a question about something negative in my life because I could recall every detail—too bad I can't FORGET about some of those things! It's not fair how this memory thing goes. Maybe that's my next book…I doubt it, because by the time I write it, I'll forget everything!

Sometimes I wish I could go back to 1969 when I was a hippie and start over again. But I know in my heart that I came back to this Earth to get some of the deeper lessons over this time around. As I look back, I feel strongly that I must have been pretty evolved spiritually to come back and experience the challenges that I've gone through.

Years ago Randy and I decided that we weren't going to have any more children after we had Jay (nothing personal Jay!). We felt blessed that our firstborn was healthy and thought it was wise to stop there. After making the decision we were content in setting other goals for ourselves. When I was pregnant with Jay, I graduated with my Master's in counseling and was excited to start working in my field. We had visions of renovating our first home, which was an older home on the south side of Youngstown. We wanted to get it ready to be sold so we could eventually move into a nicer neighborhood, etc. We had many sugarplums running through our heads at the time!

In the midst of moving forward in life, I was having some female issues. My ob-gyn said that I had a stubborn vaginal infection that wouldn't respond to treatment. He gave me a strong antibiotic as a last resort. To our surprise, it wasn't a vaginal infection. I was pregnant. We were, of course, very concerned because of medications I took in the critical days of conception. Randy and I sat down and went over the results of several clinical studies with our doctor. There was a possibility of minimal neurological risk to the fetus. *Minimal neurological risk* played over and over in my mind. We had a hard decision to make. My communication with Chris began at that point in time. It was the beginning of our strong bond and connection that we still have today.

Randy and I struggled with the idea of aborting. Well, it was mostly me who struggled. I was so frightened that something would be wrong with my baby and had clear images of how this child would be born deformed. However, as I learned much later in life, everything happens for a reason. Chris wanted to come into this world and his desire strongly overpowered my fears. Christopher Lee Burns was born on June 17, 1983 (we joked about using **diaphragm** as his middle name since that's how the blooper occurred)! Little did I know that this mighty soul would change the course of my life.

I was scheduled for a C-section but deathly afraid of delivering him. As I said, from the onset of my pregnancy, I had waves of grief that he would be born deformed. I wonder if on a soul level I knew that my time with him would be short and I didn't want to live through an ending, as strange as that sounds. Chris came out as scheduled...a little bundle of joy! He was a miracle baby. Everything that we could see and touch was in perfect order. My fear was over...or so I thought.

As Chris grew, I knew he was special. He was very sensitive. When the boys said their prayers at night, Jay prayed for a bigger bike or more toys and Chris prayed that the people in the hospitals would get well. He had a look of wisdom, compassion and depth. He had big beautiful eyes and the longest eyelashes in the world. His smile went from ear to ear. His hair, platinum as a child, was always going in eleven different directions. Every mother wants to think that their child is something divine and special, and really they all are.... They are miracles in the making. Chris was really different though.

When he was around five years old, he drew his face titled "Me I Am Special." In a dream, he asked me to include this drawing in this book.

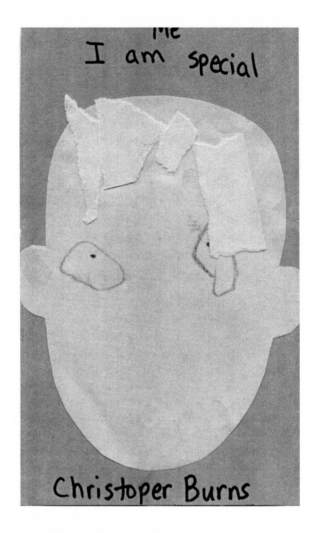

I was given a wall hanging as a baby gift that said, "God gave this child to you to guide, to love, to walk through life beside. A little child so full of charms, to fill a pair of loving arms. God picked you out because he knew how safe his child would be with you." It hung above his light switch in his room and I read it often as I turned his light out. I still read it when I need to be consoled.

When he passed away and I finally went through all of his drawers and closet, my impressions of him were reinforced. He loved the little things in life. He had a habit of putting his little "treasures" in small sandwich bags. When I went through a large chest in his closet, I found a part of a wishing bone in a bag that he probably saved for years. He had his little erasers that obviously meant something to him, and another bag with one little seashell in it. Knowing my son, he felt grateful for those things and they meant the world to him.

I'll never forget the Big Bird story. I bought him a two-foot Big Bird for his room and had it sitting on his dresser. He said to me a few days in a row when he was five that Big Bird was watching him through the night and he wanted him to stop. I told him that it was impossible because Big Bird was just a toy. He insisted that I was wrong. One morning when I went to wake him, Big Bird was not sitting up; he was bent over. When I sat him up, I realized Chris had put masking tape across his eyes. He said he had to take care of the problem because he needed to get some sleep!

During his early years, probably the most significant of many things happening to me was that my deeper sense of intuition was beginning to grow. Chris had touched my heart. I was honored to be around him because of his presence. His spirit was different than anyone I knew. He was gifted and enlightened and I knew it on a deeper level. He once told me that when he was little he knew things were going to happen before they did. As he got older and started to share his gift with his friends, he was shocked to learn that not everyone had that gift. He enjoyed spooking his dates with his predictions. *"They can't resist me, Mom!"*

Unfortunately Chris was born with some issues. He was born dyslexic...north, south, east and west. He had several learning disabilities and was diagnosed with ADD around the age of six. He received physical therapy to develop his hand-eye coordination. We had to go back to crawling when he was five because he was diagnosed with a condition called Symmetric Tonic Neck Reflex, which has to do with crawling. There is a purpose for everything and little did I know how important crawling is to a toddler. Years ago, the walkers were very popular and we put our kids in them to get a break for a few minutes. My theory is that Chris skipped the crawling stage and went right to walking because of the walker. We thought he was so precocious. Children need to crawl to suppress their neck reflex. If they don't and they lower their hand on a table to color or write, the neck reflex is triggered and the child has to attempt to keep their hand controlled. Think about how infants look when they are born. They have their fists next to their ears. As the infant learns to crawl, it suppresses the neck muscle so they can use their limbs independently of one another. This enables a child to develop good eye-hand coordination. Since Chris didn't crawl long enough, he had a difficult time doing paper and pencil tasks. When his arm was lowered to the table, he couldn't form his letters or color properly. Interestingly enough, if he sat lower than the tabletop and had to reach his arm up to reach the table, the reflex wasn't triggered and he could do tasks at hand.

Part of our nightly routine was for the two of us to crawl for several minutes. Chris struggled nightly with painful exercises. As he crawled, I had to pull on his legs to create the resistance so he could suppress the reflex properly. Once he did, we could see visible evidence of how he was able to form his alphabet, color, etc. But he had constant neck pain and headaches. It was one more bridge for him to cross and he did. It was so hard for me to create pain for him when my mission was to relieve it. I was so aware of how hard he had to try to be like everyone else and I admired his determination and strong will.

My fears of something happening to him never quieted down. During his first three years of life, I had constant nightmares of losing him. I would burst into tears, mostly when I was alone, after getting explicit images of horrible things happening to Chris. It was as though I was going through rehearsals of what was yet to come.

At the age of three he was abducted at a festival in our hometown. My sister Bonnie rescued him. He was within seconds of being gone. The elderly woman who snatched him from an amusement park ride had him to her car when Bonnie stopped her. In fact, Chris remembered two of the letters in her license plate.

Later, the police informed my mother that they felt the abduction was connected to a child pornographic ring that was under investigation. He said it was common for elderly people to get $10,000 if they abducted a child. Children were flown out of state and their identities changed. What a nightmare! My sister said the woman was very unassuming. She just looked like someone's grandmother. I'm convinced that my sister was one of Chris's Earth angels. She was there when he needed her the most. Once again, I want to thank you, Bonnie, for being there. Our lives would have changed drastically that day if the events had played out another way.

Also at the age of 6 or 7 he almost drowned in a pool when the current of a large fountain pulled him under water. My best friend at the time saved him. I was holding him but I could hardly save myself. Thank you, Sue for being there that day. I don't think he would have made it without you.

As you can imagine, my fears were off the charts at that point. Chris and I experienced separation anxiety for several months after that incident. He also came close to being abducted at the age of eight in our neighborhood. He was with his childhood friend Matt and a man stopped them as he was driving by in his car. He offered them some candy and asked them to help him find his lost dog. Thank God, both boys had enough sense to say "no" to this perpetrator. The man was eventually found.

In the midst of all of the drama surrounding Chris, I was working as a full-time therapist in private practice. I told a colleague about my high levels of anxiety over losing Chris. Ironically enough,

I had no fear whatsoever of losing Jay. This wasn't some maternal neurosis of some sort. My pregnancy was easy with Jay and raising him to that point was not difficult either. There wasn't anything about my history with Jay that could explain the constant fear of losing Chris. My colleague talked me into going to a past life training seminar in Pittsburgh, Pennsylvania for the weekend. I was intrigued and she felt that I might find my answers there. I was shocked at my experiences that weekend. Our instructor was Dr. Roger Woolger who has studied past-life regression and written several books on his findings. I had several regressions that weekend, but the most significant was the one of my life in Italy. It brought everything together for me. In that life, I was living on the streets in Italy, a true bag lady. One day I was walking around an outdoor marketplace. I was very poor, hungry and dirty. I stopped at a table and the merchant was laughing at me and calling me ugly. He held up a bottle so I could see how ugly I was. My hair was matted and my face was dirty. I was ashamed of myself. I began to cry and his very compassionate daughter tried to console me. She gave me something to eat as her father was yelling at her for even talking to me. She whispered in my ear that I should return at the end of the day and I did.

To make a long story short, she offered me a job cleaning her house. I made enough money to eventually get my own space and live with some pride and esteem. I eventually married in that life and the regression fast-forwarded to the home where my son and husband were living. I remember walking into the home with a bag of groceries. I could hear giggling as I approached the front door of my humble home. My spouse was chasing my son, who was about three, around the coffee table and they were both having lots of giggles and fun. I can clearly remember feeling such joy and being so grateful for my home and family. I walked into the kitchen to prepare dinner for them and I heard a loud thump. I ran to the doorway and saw my son lying on the floor motionless. I knew as I looked at his body that he was dead from the blow to his head. I was paralyzed in that moment with grief.

Once you are regressed and reliving the significant parts of that lifetime, you complete it by going to your death and reenacting it if necessary. As regressions go, I realized that the significant part of that life was the reunification with the soul of my child. Dr. Woolger then fast-forwarded the regression to the end of my life. I died of natural causes but when I finally passed, I was reunited with the soul of my child. He then asked me if that soul is anyone that I know today and without hesitation, I said *Chris*. I learned that at the moment of trauma or death, we carry those injuries, emotional states, fears, etc. into the next life and will play them out again until resolved. My fear of losing Chris was being played out again in this life. It made more sense to me than anything else I had discovered.

That immediately connected me to other pieces along the way that suddenly made sense to me. For example, when I was pregnant with Chris, Randy and I purchased a new home and we were moving during my eighth month of pregnancy. Randy wanted a coffee table and we argued about it. I resisted strongly, which was ONE time that I won my argument. It made sense why I was so resistant. I learned the weekend of past-life training that Chris died in his last life from hitting his head on a coffee table. Also at the moment of death, he had a blow to the head. He came into this life with neurological disabilities and his life ended due to the fact that his brain died from lack of oxygen.

From what I gathered, he died in his past life at the age of three in Italy and he could have had a near-death experience when he was abducted at an Italian festival at the age of three in this life. There are several interesting, significant parallels. I'll never know if they really mean anything but I'm choosing to believe that they do. I left that weekend knowing why I was so afraid of losing Chris. I've thought long and hard about all of this and I choose to believe that Chris is one of my teachers. He travels with me to teach me how to overcome adversity and fear and to believe in myself...against all odds.

Chris and Jay three weeks before his death. One of the last pictures ever taken of him.

Chris and his dad

Fun in the Tub

**Must see the "before and after" photo to appreciate why I
should have been nominated for mother of the year!**

Chris at his best at Jay's in Cali!

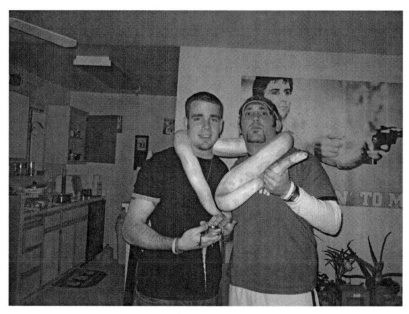

All macho and nowhere to go.....

LOOK OUT, HERE THEY COME!!!!

If any of you have children with ADD/ADHD, you'll find this chapter challenging to embrace. First of all, ADD/ADHD is neurological. We are born with it, although some have developed the symptoms from a head injury or head trauma. Both of my sons were diagnosed with ADD/ADHD. Chris was diagnosed as a child and Jay in high school. I don't feel that Jay was born with it, but he sustained several head traumas from football injuries and car accidents and developed prefrontal attention difficulties. However, with the strong strain of attention problems on both sides of the family, it wouldn't be a surprise if Jay had been born with it.

When the boys were four and six years of age,. Randy and I decided to turn the corner without each other. We tried hard to make our marriage work, but we are so different. Besides, we had fundamental religious differences that we couldn't manage. I'm Catholic and he's the devil! (Just kidding of course.) That was a difficult and very sad time in our lives. I wasn't sure how life was going to go without Randy around but I also knew that we would have to find a way to make it without him. I still don't know how I avoided developing some sort of an addiction. If anyone needed to block reality, it was me! God obviously gave me a strong constitution and, as I've said before, everything happens for a reason.

Some parts of my childhood clearly were significant in that I learned how to be patient, tolerant, persevere and let go of the things that made me cry. I learned to study more, laugh and find joy in music. I cried when no one was looking. So I guess the difficult times as a small child prepared me for life as an adult. I was never afraid to climb a mountain, even if I had to do it alone. When left alone, I have a very effective way of finding my smile and entertaining myself. It is my salvation. God never creates blueprints that are bloopers and he did a fine job with mine. I've often said I wish I could meet someone just like me!

There were times when the three of us could have appeared on the Jerry Springer show. There was constant fighting between the boys. Chris's delayed reactions and responses annoyed Jay. It was not unusual for the word "retard" to be heard in our home, and OFTEN on a bad day, *Candid Camera* could have caught me walking around with my headset on, trying to block the constant noise. There was continuous movement and noise. I don't know which was worse. I had an egg timer on my counter and when I thought of it I would ask Chris to refrain from talking until all of the sand hit the bottom. It NEVER happened. His favorite word was why. *Why do I have to? Why did you say that? Why does a bird chirp? Why are the clouds white? Why aren't teeth round?* And on and on and on he went, just like the energizer bunny. Chris was curious about everything.

The scary thing for me was when he was quiet and staring at something or someone for an extended period of time. If he stared long enough, I knew he was going to ask a question and usually his voice was loud and squeaky. We had an electrician working on

46

the house, and when she said her name was Kim, I caught Chris staring and I was trying to distract him before the words flew out of his mouth. But I wasn't quick enough. Out came, *"Why does that man have a girl's name?"*

And then there were tender moments, and there were many. I'll never forget when he was five and listening to one of my close friends practice a song on the keyboard. He later asked me why water runs out of his eyes when he listens to Sue play music. I was very touched by his innocence and as he grew, music became a very important part of his life. When he wanted me to understand where he was in life, he would ask me to listen to a song with him. Both boys have always shared their songs with me. Jason made me a CD of all of his favorites that I still listen to today. Music has connected us in spirit on many occasions since there were many times when we were unable to be together. Another tender moment was when he was around six and he wanted me to make Christmas cookies for our elderly neighbors. He saved some money and wanted to buy them a gift because he was sad that they would be alone. It was not unusual for me to find him sitting on their porches talking their ears off. I bet he brought them hours of joy, unless of course they turned their hearing aids down when they saw him walking up the driveway!

There were many challenging moments, too. There was the time we went to buy fireworks and just when I took my eyes off of them for a minute, they were in the brush behind the building gathering up every snake they could find. They got in the backseat without me seeing their hands full of long thin snakes. When I did realize what they had, Jerry Springer would have paid me BIG bucks for the replay! There was never ever a dull moment! At times I wondered if I would make it, but I just turned fifty-seven, so never say never!

Chris got the obsession with "Why?" from me. I can get caught in that cycle and many times I've asked God why He gave me such a challenge in life. If I'm mindful enough, I can find the answers within myself. When I ask that question I always get the same answer: *Why not? You are ready for it; it's time for you to grow.* Many years ago, I had a very bad Mother's Day. Jay was giving me such a hard time, as he often did. I just couldn't be around him that day. I hit rock bottom and asked my parents to pick the boys up and take them to dinner with the family because I needed to be alone. I was clearly having a meltdown that day. I felt like God expected me to be a machine and I was mad at Him that day. I got in my car and drove to a nearby community that has a large lake. I pulled over and sat for a few hours crying my eyes out. I had one of those conversations with God that day. I yelled but he didn't yell back. I swore but He didn't swear back. I called Him stupid for giving me children and He listened quietly. At one point though, in anger, I asked him WHY I just can't have normal kids that I can enjoy and love. If God can talk, I know I heard him say... *"It is not for your children to love you; it is for you to love yourself."* There was nothing more to say or do that day but to go home and start over and I did. I never forgot those powerful words. Did I hear them or didn't I? Who knows and who cares. It straightened out my attitude for a long while and I put that day on my gratitude list forever.

The ADHD was clearly a challenge for me. I probably would have been mother of the year if I would have taken Prozac but for some reason I hung in there without altering myself with medication. Like I said, I'm not sure how I escaped without developing some type of "ism". However, I am a fan of natural supplements like vitamins and herbs. Yet there were days that if I attached an IV to my arm with every supplement that I could afford, I was still going down!

My nature is to let things go quickly and roll with the punches. The other thing that helped is that I need very little to survive and I got adjusted to –just that: little time for me, little privacy, little sleep, little bit of money in the bank, little bit of help around the house, etc. When I say I'm a survivor, I really mean that. I'm proud of it too. But it's double-edged for me as of the time of this writing. I still need very little so when people want to share life with me, it doesn't take much for me to turn them down. I don't need anyone or anything so that ended up being one of my weaknesses. On the flip side, if the boys just gave me a hug or I heard them giggling or either one of them walked in the room with their shirt tail hanging out, zipper down, shoes untied and hair going in eleven different directions, it was plenty for me to recuperate from a difficult day. As I said, my past prepared me to climb mountains alone... big ones.

The boys were so opposite that it was impossible for them to get along when they were younger. When Chris was around twelve, he said to me one day, "*I don't care anymore if Jay doesn't like me or thinks I'm stupid. It doesn't bother me anymore, Mom. Don't worry about me. I'm OK now.*"

I can't tell you what a relief that was for me to hear. I felt that Chris would be damaged for life because of how his brother treated him, but everyone who watched them reminded me that someday they would be best friends. I had no tolerance for it. If Jay called Chris a retard, it would hurt me. Or, if I saw them fight, I would be scared to death of someone getting injured. My father would say, "*Just let them go. They are just boys and that's how they act.*" Well, if anything sounded retarded to me, it was comments like those. I was insistent that they didn't have to act like buttholes every minute of every day. I still think that way. Why do men have to act the way they do? Now I immediately say, "*Who cares?*" I've made a living as a counselor because of their behavior!

Chris seemed to need his brother's approval and acceptance; sadly enough, he wanted to *be* Jay and knew that he never could. He was always twenty minutes behind the ball and Jay was twenty minutes in front of it. When Chris was heavily into his addiction and looking for employment, he left a resume on the computer screen. It made me cry because he actually copied most of Jay's resume. It dawned on me that Chris didn't know who he was. I told him that he was much, much greater than the words on a resume. I tried to assure him that he was the sweetest guy I had ever met and I hoped that someday every woman in the world could be with a man like him because they would think they had died and gone to heaven. He was charming, funny, bright but humble, generous and thoughtful, but very lazy! I blamed the ADD for the laziness. But here is where the twist occurs.

I have learned to appreciate ADD for its strengths, not judge it for its weaknesses. It was always difficult to get Chris where he needed to be unless he was internally motivated. Then it wasn't an issue at all. When he wanted to get up to go fishing or get to a friend's house to play Madden or meet some "hot" girl, he was in the shower and a few minutes early. He had no problem staying focused, getting started, finishing what he set out to do. Chris's gift in being ADD was that he could only be in the moment. He didn't worry about later because it didn't exist in his world. His innate ability to capture detail and share it is something I miss. One starry summer night, he was yelling up to my bedroom window, *"Ma get down here! You are missing this!"* I was in the middle of something but decided to drop it and go outside. He was so thrilled that he picked me up and twirled me around and then he pointed out all of the constellations. He wanted me to see the Big Dipper and the North Star. I'm really in the dark with all of that so I was impressed. But remember, his lips were moving so he could have been lying for all I know. It was a night I'll never forget. He was childlike and smiling from ear to ear. He made sounds like a whistle when he was excited and I'm sure he was heard through the neighborhood since it was a still summer night. Later that night when I got into bed, I thanked God for sending me this ray of light. *Thank you my little love. When I look up on a starry night, I'll always feel you in my heart.*

His ADHD made life very interesting for everyone. Trying to keep him on task was a chore that I wasn't successful with most of the time. One year he was so excited to get the Christmas lights hung on the roof. He asked me to get them all ready for him to hang, so I did. Next thing I know I hear him running from one end of the roof to the other…back and forth. *"What the hell is he doing up there?"* I went outside and yelled up at him. He came to the highest point on the roof with a bandana on and as he slowly raised his head, I saw that he was pointing his bb gun at me. He yelled down, *"Who wants to know?"* He looked like Rambo and admitted to shooting at the street signs. That was another one of those days where I just walked away, shaking my head and humming the song, *"Nobody Knows the Trouble I've Seen, Nobody Knows But Jesus!"*

I loved when he told stories about his day. He had a huge heart and wanted to make everyone smile. One day he came home after a job interview. I asked him how it went and he immediately told me about the older woman who was struggling with the groceries as she was crossing the street. He pulled his car over and helped her, getting her safely to her car. He was hired but never boasted about how well the interview went. The only thing he said was that the man who interviewed him witnessed his behavior and said that he was the kind of man he wanted working for him. He always said the same thing, *"They loved me!"* I knew he got the job because the first day of work, they called the home and asked for him because he never showed up. He was in Florida vacationing! Unbelievable!

The truth is everyone who knew him loved him. He made us all feel special. It was his gift to us. I was telling my sister Cookie that Chris clearly came to this Earth teaching us how to forgive and let go. It was impossible to stay upset with him, even if he stole from you, lied to you, cheated on you or beat you up. He loved us and we knew it deep in our hearts and because of the power of LOVE, we could forgive and accept him and all of his weaknesses. He was so humble and never wanted to be center stage, but would proudly sit back and watch the rest of us do our thing. When Jay graduated from law school and his name was called, Chris was filming him and the camera was bouncing all over the place. All I could hear was Chris screaming, *"That's my bro!"*

I'm a percussion player and when he was able to see me play in the band I was in, he whistled and smiled from ear to ear. He couldn't quit taking pictures and was so proud of me. Chris never once tried to steal someone's moment from them.

When he was eleven, he begged me to get him a dog. He promised to clean up after the dog and of course we all know how that would go. I decided to get an eight-month-old golden retriever. When we went to see the dog, they fell instantly in love with each other. Her name was Ginger and she jumped right up on Chris and as he fell back, he yelled out, *"She's awesome, Mom! I want her!"* From that day forward he adored Ging. She was a big dog. At her heaviest she weighed in at 118 lbs. He loved to wrestle with her, pick her up and twirl her around. When he put her down and she was dizzy, he would laugh uncontrollably. They were so much fun to watch. Chris used Ging to get around punishments. If I would send him to his room, he would try to do something to get me to laugh so I would drop the punishment. My favorite was when he would send Ging into the room with his favorite hat on, which he referred to as his "fursillia" and he would talk for her as she would walk into the room. *"Mom, don't make me bite you! You are being very mean to Chris and you need to be nicer!"*

When Ginger was diagnosed with cancer, he couldn't come to terms with the fact that she was going to die. This was three years before Chris passed away and her prognosis was poor. The vet said she had maybe a year but that the cancer was aggressive and he couldn't get it all.

I think most of us have read the Chicken Soup For Animal Lovers and how our little Earth angels wait until it's right for us before they go. Ging sat near me as I cried for Chris. She held hands with me. She cried with me. She gave me kisses when I sat alone and when she leaned up against me with her frail aging body, she hugged me as hard as she could. But I could see it in her eyes that she needed to go. One night I sat on the floor with her and thanked her for being my best friend and for waiting for me to get stronger. I told her it was time for her to go to Chris if she needed to and that I would be OK. It wasn't even the cancer that took her from me; she slipped on the ice a few weeks later and ruptured her two back ACLs. She waited for ten months after Chris died to go. It was another time in life where I couldn't catch my breath from crying. But they are together again and that is what makes it so tolerable for me. I knew as I was holding her head in my arms when she died, that Chris was there holding us both in his.

When I walked into my empty house the first night that Ginger was put to sleep, I felt so alone. I felt like I was walking around a furniture store: my children were gone, and my little love Ging too. It was the first time in my life that I didn't want to be alive anymore. I didn't want to live another day. My life as I knew it was over; it would never be the same. I couldn't imagine ever being OK with the silence.

As I forced myself to walk through the rooms and sit in my backyard alone, I was rewinding the precious moments in my life. I deeply missed hearing Ging's nails on the hardwood floors; I missed hearing the garage door open and someone walk into the back door; I missed hearing my boys fighting with each other; I wanted to hear Chris and Steph giggling in the family room; Ging barking to go out; stereos and TVs blasting; Jay and Chris's friends raiding the junk food cabinet. I needed to fall in the toilet in the middle of the night; pick up Jay's dirty socks off the kitchen counter; smell cologne in the bathroom; see a cigarette butt on the garage floor; step in gum and spit on the driveway; I needed to hear laughter and fighting over Madden games; Chris jumping on my waterbed until I got up to cook him breakfast; bundle up and make hot chocolate for the football games; lay on the trampoline in the backyard and count the clouds; get under the covers with flashlights and read a book; get squirted in the back of my head with a squirt gun; sit in the car and hold my breath when one of them passed gas; smell Johnson's baby powder after they were squeaky clean; watch them sleeping in their beds; pinch their bums as they run up the stairs giggling; and pile all three of us on the Honda Spree to buzz around the field in our backyard. I would give anything to hear Ging bark one more time and Chris say, *"Ma, I'm hungry. Cook me up some grub!"* My life will never be the same. I get so sick when I revisit the bottom of my heart.

What I have now are clear images of Chris and Ging lying on a couch together somewhere over the rainbow where I believe the true land of the living exists.

THE TWO FACES OF ADDICTION

This chapter is very difficult for me to write. I am sticking to what I believe in and I know that there is some purpose and meaning for Chris's addiction. It's hard for me to really know when it all began. As I think about the sequence of medical/health issues in his life, I can blame it on that, but in my heart I know that there really is no one or nothing to blame. It was part of the journey we had to walk with him. Each of us has to decide what it meant and how it was valuable to our own personal and spiritual growth. When he was in his first treatment program in the summer of 2003, he ended a part of his journal with this:

> 6/13 *PPPS The sad thing is that if I didn't break my back, this never would of happened. I used to take a pain pill here and there but mostly from all of my surgeries. I NEVER did or would of took Oxys if I didn't break my back and that makes me furious.*

Chris was always happy and hopeful in life. His vision was to be a counselor. Because of his learning disabilities and ADD everything was harder for him but he was very determined to be a good student and wanted us to be proud of him. It was difficult to follow in Jay's footsteps. Jay has always achieved everything that he set out to do and never could understand what Chris experienced on a daily basis. I don't think any of us could; he protected us from knowing how deeply he struggled.

Life changed for us in the fall of his senior year. He was so excited to play football that year. He wanted to show Jay how well he could play. Jay had many accolades for his scholastic and athletic abilities. Chris just stood in the distance smiling and cheering for his brother.

He worked hard to get in shape and couldn't wait to start the season. Unfortunately, the last practice before the first game of the season, he was tackled by a freshman who hit Chris's knee with his helmet. He tore his ACL and meniscus, which required knee surgery. This was one of the pivotal times in his life. He became very depressed when he couldn't play ball his senior year. His threshold for pain was low as it was because of the ADD, and with the depression; he wasn't a very good patient during his recovery. He was asking for more pain pills but his physician at the time refused to give him more than he felt he needed for that type of injury and recovery. It was difficult for me to see him as a depressed young man. It was something that I had never seen before in Chris.

The first game of the season was heartbreaking for all of us. As his team ran out on the field, he walked across it on crutches and stood on the sidelines, where he remained throughout the entire season. I admired the courage it took for him to walk out there for every game to support his team. It might sound like such a small event in the whole scheme of things, but I do think that it weakened his spirit. This was the first time I was aware of how hard it was for him to find his courage and strength to keep on going. Typically people suffering from depression experience mood changes and anger, which is a good way to describe Chris during that time. He was difficult to be around at times. He fought more with Stephanie and seemed to distance somewhat from us all.

When football season ended, things eventually got better for him. It seemed like the old Chris was back. No one was playing ball so he was back in the flow of adolescence with all of his friends. In a blink he was graduating and going off to college at Mount Union in Ohio. He often said that the summer of 2002 was the best summer ever. He was feeling better and looking forward to spending time with his friends knowing that everyone was going their separate ways by the end of summer. I wasn't sure how things would go for Chris and Steph. He adored her but most of the time you wouldn't have known it because they fought a lot. Stephanie will always hold a special place in my heart because she was always there for him when she could be. She put up with more than any young girl would have.

That summer was not what he expected it to be. In June, Chris was in a car accident on the way to work. Someone drove left of the center and he swerved to avoid an accident. His car hit a pole and hydroplaned and rolled several times, landing on its roof. From what we could surmise, Chris hit his head and when he came to, he told us that he heard the engine hissing and was terrified that his car was going to blow up. He broke a window and crawled out. He had several cuts and injuries but it was a miracle that they weren't worse.

He remembers being in excruciating pain as he crawled through a field to get to the street. If that wasn't bad enough, he wasn't aware that he crawled through poison ivy and had an outbreak of that as well. He lay on the street with a bloody face and head while several cars drove by and never stopped. His angel that day was an elderly woman who took the time to stop and call for help. We never did get her name to thank her, as she left before the police and ambulance arrived. We found out later that Chris broke his lower back in that accident and had other minor injuries. I was very concerned because he hadn't fully recovered from the knee surgery. His knee was often swollen, affecting how he walked and putting pressure on his back. With the fractured back, it was going to be a bigger challenge for him.

He was given painkillers to help with the back pain and other injuries. His depression got a little worse but he was still fighting to keep his spirits high. He argued about going on an antidepressant. He felt he was going to be fine especially since he was going to start college and "*I know my luck is going to change, Mom.*" However, he was limited as to what he could do and fought more with all of us. He was going to physical therapy for his back, but it was getting closer to orientation at Mount Union and he wasn't released from physical therapy. He insisted on starting college with all of his friends, trying to explain to me that if he didn't start school with everyone else it would be one more disappointment for him. *How could I not understand that?* He asked.

The physical therapist felt that he was going to need to continue with therapy but not as often and Chris agreed to drive home for his treatments. It was a plan! Chris also assured us that he would wear the back brace given to him. My gut feeling was that he was not going to wear it since it looked like a turtle shell. I knew he would be embarrassed but he assured me that if he didn't wear it he wouldn't be able to walk around campus because of the back discomfort. Special accommodations were made for housing and his classes and it all seemed doable.

I was so proud of him for being as determined and dedicated to start college. He felt he could do it and that I was worrying needlessly, but I was still uncomfortable with the timing. I didn't want to be a doting mother and doubt his ability to overcome difficult circumstances because he had a proven track record of being strong and courageous. I was confident that if the plan went as discussed, everything would turn out fine.

So what do you think happened next, ladies? You bet! We shopped til we dropped! He had everything he needed to make his new home comfortable and fun and I was onboard with the excitement. As always, I got those pangs in my belly that I often tried to ignore thinking I was being like my mother, a worrywart. I often reminded my sister to shoot me if I turned out like my mother; more often than not she reminds me that it's time for her to load her gun. I guess it's just part of the gene pool, that and the wide hips and mustache. Que sera, sera!

The day Jay and I dropped Chris off at Mount Union was bittersweet. He was so scared and nervous which was to be expected of course. Jay and I helped him set up his room and we had our usual laughs. Jay joked that Chris had to find a real skinny girl to sleep with since he was a "fat load" and he only had a single mattress. Leave it to Jay to fill in with the hardcore facts as often as he could!

The day was fun for the three of us and the time to say goodbye arrived much too quickly. I wanted to be excited and strong for him but shed tears for different reasons. I wasn't crying so much out of happiness as I was out of concern. He had needed so much guidance and help through the years. No one knew that as much as the two of us, and I wondered how he was going to fare on his own. I kept a lot of his fears and insecurities from Jay and Randy because they would make fun of him and call him a "Mama's boy that was hanging onto the apron strings." It was very important for him to graduate from college. I have two Master's degrees and his brother was determined to earn a Jurist Doctorate from Golden Gate University of Law in San Francisco.

During all of this, Jay was home for his summer break from John Carroll University. He was getting ready to go back and I wasn't sure what the house would be like without the two of them, but I didn't have to worry about finding out either! When Chris started school he was home more than not. I'd come home from work to find him on the couch with Ging next to him. This, of course, was after he raided the fridge! He'd laugh and say Ging called him on his cell and asked him to come home and watch TV with her. *"It's the truth, Mom!"* Those precious lips were moving again but I loved his humor, and of course I loved that he missed home.

However as the year progressed I saw a difference in him, and was hoping it was normal adjustment. He called less and hardly came home, which wasn't like Chris. He loved sharing his experiences with me in detail. Jay is the same way, except every piece of the bloody detail. One thing I did notice was how nervous Chris was when he came home for visits. He ran up and down the steps to his bedroom, out the front door, in the back door, eating lots of sweets, and drinking tons of Gatorade and Mountain Dew. He couldn't look at me and talked while he was moving, usually past me and out the door. Again, I wanted to believe that he was growing up and this was the new (but not improved) Chris. I wanted to believe that he was letting go of me, which was what I hoped for him at some point in time. We both needed to let go. I certainly don't want you to think that my life revolved around him because while all of this was going on I was running a business, seeing clients full time and taking care of a home, dog and a commercial building. There were always many things going on at once.

We got through that first year but not without a glitch. He was accused in February 2003 of going into the wrestling locker room on campus and stealing around twenty dollars. Due to the fact that he wasn't a wrestler and had no reason to be in the locker room, Mount Union was charging him with breaking and entering and minor theft. Chris was so upset because he said he didn't steal the money and we would see that he was telling the truth once the locker room tapes were played in the courtroom. Sure enough that day in court, the tape showed

> Chris, I haven't been able to stop thinking of you...asking why this disease is so cunning, baffling and powerful...why.... you? (www.myspace.com/burnz2)

him entering the locker room and opening up three lockers but not stealing anything from them. He turned around and smiled at us because he knew he was innocent. We were all relieved when we saw the tape. However, it didn't play out that way. This ridiculous case went before the grand jury where he was found guilty of a felony based upon one wrestler's testimony. He was suspended from school and things got much worse. I knew there was something wrong but didn't know what. I asked Jay if he thought Chris was on drugs and he assured me that he wasn't, so I tried to let it go but couldn't. Things were turning up missing. One day I came home from work and noticed that an heirloom that was passed down to me after my father died was gone, as was other gold jewelry. Chris listened to me for hours trying to solve the mystery. I called the cleaning lady and family members to ask if they were in the house until I finally concluded that I had to call the police and report the theft. It was then that Chris told me that his friend had been in my room that day and he would find out if he took the jewelry.

The next morning, some of the jewelry showed up on the kitchen counter, with an apology note. He asked me not to involve the police because his friend was very sorry. I believed him. I'm sure you know what I'm going to say next. Yes, things continued to get worse. He finally admitted to being addicted to drugs. He said that one of the students on campus handed him an OxyContin when he learned he was in pain from a broken back. *"I felt like a young guy again. I had no pain and I was hooked after the first one. If I would have known all of this was going to happen, I would have never taken that first Oxy,"* he said.

Chris admitted that he was addicted and wanted help. He agreed to go into his first treatment program in the summer of 2003. He was admitted to Glenbeigh Hospital in Rock Creek, Ohio where he stayed for thirty days. Everyone was so proud of him. He was so frightened but very sick by then and really wanted help.

We loved him so much and felt like our prayers were answered and everything would be all right. When we pulled into Glenbeigh, it felt like we were going before a firing squad, until Chris saw a friend that I later discovered was his dealer. Some of the tension lifted when they started talking and the boy told Chris that he was going to like it there and it was helping him. I felt like we were doing the right thing. He hugged me so hard and asked me not to give up on him. How could I ever do that? It was impossible for me.

The Glenbeigh stay was good for Chris. While he was in detox, we were not permitted to have any contact. He sent me a few pages from his journal, and I could hear the signs of recovery and hope in his words. He had a ton of support from family and friends. This was such a hopeful time for us; it was obvious that he was gaining some self-confidence and respect back. We went up every Sunday for family day and saw such an improvement in a few weeks.

We seemed to be on the right track. He was discharged after thirty days and felt as though he had turned the bend permanently. Chris had a spiritual awakening in Glenbeigh. When my father died in 2000, I gave him his Italian gold horn to hang from his neck chain. When I noticed it missing, he said he lost it, but I assumed that it was sold for drug money. The day he got out of detox and was moved onto the floor where he would stay, he said he was putting his things in his closet and laid his cigarettes and bandana on the bed. He said when he went to get them after he finished setting up his room; the Italian gold charm was lying in the center of the bandana. He cried when he shared the story with me. He felt that God had blessed him that day and his grandpa was trying to tell him that he was supporting him. It was amazing how strong Chris's beliefs were. It was a clear example of how much power our beliefs have (good or bad) over how we feel. When we choose to find the good in the moment, We will feel so much better even if it's for a few moments. Why not, I ask?

Chris was feeling very strong, or so I thought. Now, he had to get through the probation period from the felony conviction, eventually get his record expunged and we believed he would be on his way, chemically free and ready to get back to real life. What we were taught in Glenbeigh was "once an addict always an addict." I clearly got that but I don't think Chris did. Returning to Mount Union in the fall was not an option so he signed up for school at Youngstown State University, closer to home, to continue his major in social work.

Moving his things out of Mount Union was hard for him because it was a reminder of how drug abuse had impacted his life so quickly and easily. He was living at home and going to class but not working. He spent most of his time at home and away from parties and his friends who were still using drugs. He seemed to be serious about staying away from drugs and out of trouble. However, he didn't have much of a life and that concerned me also. I wondered if he could stay away from using once he began to socialize again. I heard more often than not, *"Ma, don't worry about me. I'm all right."* It also concerned me that he wasn't going to meetings and he didn't have a sponsor. He didn't feel like he needed to. *"I'm really not an addict, Mom. It just happened. I'm not like the rest of them. I'm fine."*

By Christmas of 2003 he thought he could handle seeing some of his friends and decided to go to some holiday parties. He disclosed to me a few months later that he went to a party and someone handed him an OxyContin pill, *"and that was all it took for me, Mom. I felt like in about one week, that I was living the nightmare again."* He was very edgy, eating tons of sweets, talking fast or not talking at all and avoiding us. I could tell that he wasn't going to school. He took out his student loan for the second half of the year but never even bought a book. He obviously used his loan money for drugs. He did manage to do his social work internship at my center and had permission to work under my supervision and under a social worker in practice with me. We concurred that he was very insightful and good with the clients. He was calm and very pleasant. He treated them with compassion. He appeared to genuinely enjoy the role of a counselor and I knew in my heart that he would be an extraordinary addictions counselor/social worker. Chris and I discussed that he'd take over my caseload once I went into semi-retirement.

In 1996 I built a commercial building to start a holistic health center. He was so excited about the venture; he felt like it was a guarantee for him to have the kind of life that he wanted. The center grew against all odds in our community. I offered mental health services in addition to workshops, drumming and yoga, different forms of exercise classes, massage, Reiki, hypnosis, acupuncture and chiropractic services. It was way ahead of its years in Mahoning County. In the back of my mind, it was Chris's future in mental health. I could lay that foundation for him and he would do the rest. But my mind was not at peace. One morning during his social work supervision, he appeared to be falling asleep. It was confusing for me because as I looked over and thought he was asleep, which totally infuriated me, he would make a comment or ask a question that was perfectly timed and appropriate. I wondered why he couldn't hold his head up but he assured me that he was OK. He pretended to be writing notes.

You can pretty much guess how things progressed. It really is so predictable when an addict is in denial. He pawned the computer that I bought him, my binoculars and some other personal items. I would probably be shocked if I knew all of what he did during those couple of months. I'm actually glad I don't know. That is the sad thing about drug addiction: addicts are known to turn to crime for their drug. He was starting to get lost and disconnected. Stephanie and Chris broke up for good by now and I think that was a very pivotal time for him. He felt strongly that the three people who he could always count on were Jay, Steph and I. Steph was out of the equation now.

I knew it was a matter of time and we would be confronting him to go back into treatment. A few months later, I received a call at the office from his close friend who informed me that Chris stole $600 from his brother's room that day and was denying it. I was so upset that I left work early to talk to him. He didn't expect me home and was sitting in the garage having a cigarette with his best friend Billy. The way he was leaning on his legs with his elbows, I was able to clearly see the bruises on his inner arms from the needle marks. I don't know how to describe that moment. It was almost surreal, something that you see in a movie. I couldn't believe that my son was using needles. I couldn't even find my words. My mind went blank and it took a few minutes for everything to get on the same page. I called his father and we got together to do another intervention and his attitude was different. He wanted to go into treatment but not to get well; he just knew he was in trouble and this would buy some time for a few months.

His father drove him to treatment the following morning. Once again, he seemed to respond quickly. He seemed so much happier and relaxed in treatment. He actually enjoyed it and loved helping the other patients in the program. His natural instinct to counsel seemed to shine through when he was hospitalized. But the others would distract him from his own issues. He said all of the right things, but one problem that we had in every treatment program, especially the Teen Challenge, was the constant argument that he needed to take medication for his ADHD. They felt that he needed to be off everything, including medication for a diagnosis made when he was a child. Chris could never control his impulses without it. Of course looking at his own personal issues of addiction would be more difficult for Chris than someone without ADD/HD. Chris could easily get lost in someone else's issues and get reinforced for it because he was a natural born counselor. But this was critical for his recovery. He had to stay focused on the fact that he was an addict and would always be an addict.

To prove my point, one particular night in the aftercare program, the group was meeting for family night. I went to support him and get the help I needed and he wasn't there. He went to a job interview that day at a strip bar. They hired him on the spot and started training him. When he finally got to the meeting the group leader confronted him on why he was late. He was thrilled to share with the group that he had been hired as a bouncer in a strip bar. He went on to say that the strippers would tip him and he heard he would make a lot of money. He was smiling from ear to ear like he had won the lottery. He didn't see a thing wrong with being in a bar as a recovering drug addict. When the group jumped him for being in denial, he later called them a bunch of a**holes and said they were jealous because they didn't get the job. He just didn't get it and couldn't stay focused on his program. We all tried to help him, but he stayed in denial until he was close to his death.

The time flew and he was released from probation for the felony conviction at Mount Union. He registered for Youngstown State's second semester only to get the student loan money so he could move to Florida. When he was discharged from aftercare, he still didn't go to meetings but was very careful about not going anywhere or with anyone that could lead to a relapse. I didn't know that he was in contact with a close friend who had relocated to Florida and bought a home. Chris and his friend were excited: His friend felt that it would be a fresh start for Chris and since he was clean, he could get him a well-paying job. The thought of him leaving was bittersweet for me. I was frightened for his recovery yet I wanted him to feel good about starting over with friends that he promised were clean and would be a great influence on him. He had no money but knew he would make a lot of money waiting tables. His buddy set up an interview for him at the Naples Tomato restaurant and he flew to Florida with the most excitement and hope that I had seen in him in years. He was thrilled when they offered him the job! It is a very upscale restaurant in a beautiful plaza. He showed me pictures of the home where he would be living and pictures of the restaurant. It really did seem like a dream come true for him. He was so hopeful and kept saying that God and my father had parted the clouds for him to finally start a whole new life. He said he prayed for a break and since he was blessed to have one he would NEVER go back to the life that he knew as an addict. He packed up everything that was important to him—well, everything that could possibly fit in my father's clunker, which he inherited.

I could tell that Chris was very nervous about leaving. This would be his first time so far away from home. He said he needed to grow up and that was how he planned on doing it. His buddy seemed to be doing so well for himself and really seemed to have Chris's best interests in mind. The day he was to leave Youngstown, we had a bad snowfall and the roads weren't very good. He kept on putting off leaving and before we knew it, it was time for us to go to bed. Several times during the evening he said, *"I'm leaving now, Mom,"* and we would walk toward the garage door and he would say, *"Well maybe I'll wait a little longer to see if it stops snowing."* I knew he was afraid to go alone but it was something that I knew he needed to do. I saw that little boy who just wanted me to take his hand and squeeze it tightly so he could feel better. It was almost 11 when he decided to wait and leave in the morning. I never made a bed up so fast in my life. I can't explain how relieved I was. It felt like denial to me in a sense. Deciding to stay the night felt like he decided against leaving. When I got into bed and heard him shut his bedroom door, my heart felt so light. I fell right into sleep and before I knew it, he was knocking to tell me to get up because he was leaving.

He actually got into the car with hardly any room to move and pulled out of the driveway. The tears were streaming down my cheeks as I watched him drive away. He honked several times and waved at me and yelled out the window that he loved me...and drove away. I was sobbing uncontrollably. I stood in the driveway for a while expecting him to change his mind. I began to compulsively clean, emptying ashtrays and washing his sheets, towels and any clothes he left on his bedroom floor. I gathered everything that he left behind that reminded me of him put it in his room and closed the door. *"I'll deal with that later."* I really expected the garage door to open. I really thought Chris would change his mind. It took me weeks to stop listening for the garage door at night. One night I thought I heard him yell out my name and I ran down the steps to find no one. Before he left that day, he wrote me a note and left it on my dresser. I read his note over and over. I wanted desperately to believe him. I prayed for him many times during the day and put him on several prayer lists. It was not uncommon to read requests from me asking the community to pray for him and for Jay and me so we could stay strong for one another.

> Mom,
>
> I just want to thank you. Without you I would be nothing. Your there for me every time I needed someone. Thank you for always believing in me, that is real comforting to know that someone does. I love you and I will be in touch all the time. To good times, success and a better future —
>
> I love you,
> Chris

My boys had a habit of sitting in the garage on wooden folding chairs for hours at night to talk and smoke. Whenever their friends came to hang out, all of them sat in the garage rather than sitting in our beautiful backyard on comfortable chairs. When Jay left for college, Chris left the two chairs in the garage with a pack of Jay's cigarettes on the seat where Jay usually sat. I knew when he was feeling better because he folded it up and put it away. When he went out to smoke alone and sat for long periods thinking, I knew how badly he needed to move on and make a life for himself…and I needed to do the same. It broke my heart to fold that last chair up and put it away. Still today, I feel the pain clear in the bottom of my heart when I think about that image. My most tender memories were to look out and hear them laughing and talking for hours on end. Only God knows how deeply Jay and I miss those times in our life. It seems so long ago, like it existed in another life for me.

Chris's drive down to Florida entertained me as he gave me a blow by blow description of the a**hole who tried to drive him off the road with his fancy- mobile, the girls who wanted him in the rest stops, the engine that started smoking on the car, the accidents he drove by, the morning after sleeping all night in the car, the blue skies, the night skies, the mullets that the birds had in West Virginia, the first sight of the ocean. "Ma, this is amazing. The sun is coming up and the water is so calm." He also told me about the tan that he was getting from hanging his arm out the window when he shed his winter coat and rolled the windows down for good. When he finally got to his friends house, I heard the car horn honking and him yelling, "Hey bro…what's up?" Then came, "Gotta go now, Mom. Woo hooo! Talk to you later. I love you!!" I knew it would be a while before I heard from him again, but not a long while. He loved to share his life with me when it was good. He protected me from knowing when it wasn't. That's what I loved about him being ADD. When he was overly focused on detail, he was like a little kid in a candy store. It was impossible to not share in his excitement.

The first few weeks flew by and our prayers appeared to be answered. When he called home he was excited, hopeful, humorous and really enjoying life. He repeated often how he loved his job, the space he was living in and the "hot girl" who liked him. It felt like we truly turned a bend and there was no going back to that dark and scary past. He had contacted the Bureau of Vocational Rehabilitation in Florida to get back to college and was hoping to start up in the fall. I could feel myself relaxing more and more each day. Jay was doing well in law school in California and Chris was finally getting the break he needed. He was deep-sea fishing, playing poker, swimming, enjoying the good Floridian lifestyle! He said he was going to meetings and doing it differently this time. He truly sounded like a different guy when he called home, which was often.

I started to live my life again, something that I hadn't done for a few years. I joined a female rock band with some friends and we rehearsed twice a week until we were ready to get out and start playing some gigs. It was a fun time for me. I'm a percussion player and really enjoyed myself. I felt like I could sleep again and focus on my business, which had been put on the back burner. I enjoyed waking up in the morning with a smile on my face and singing in the shower. Life was good!

Chris begged me to take a trip to Florida for my birthday and Mother's Day in May of 2004. I was thrilled to spend Mother's Day with him since I was going to spend Easter with Jay in California. *Wow, this is the life! Kids are great and I'm a traveling mom....* yep, I was blessed! The calls were coming less often but again I was accepting that he was adjusting and letting go. Could this be real?

My flight was arranged and I couldn't wait to see him! Jay and I spent so much of our time and energy on Chris, as all families do when someone close is addicted. I still wonder how Jay concentrated in law school with the constant drama. I can see, though, how Jay is now addicted to drama. If there isn't any, he has a tendency to create it because his system is so conditioned to high levels of stimulation and fear. He appears to get bored without it now, one of those consequences from living a long life of too much stress.

Law school was enough yet he took on the daily task of keeping his brother in check. Jay is a brilliant guy and he deserves to be happy. I hope the day comes very soon for him.

During our frequent phone calls, Chris assured me that he had a surprise for me on my birthday. "I can't wait, Ma. You are going to be so happy when I take you where we are going." He insisted that it remain a sacred secret until then. The day finally arrived and when I turned the bend in the airport terminal and saw him standing at the gate, I felt like someone punched me in the stomach. It was 9:30 in the evening but he had his sunglasses on. He was extremely nervous, tense, talked quickly and hugged me quickly. He told me to get my luggage and he would pull the car up, but I was standing out on the sidewalk for several minutes and he never pulled up. In fact he walked up to the sidewalk where I was standing and we walked to the car together. The airport was very small and the parking lot was compact. When I asked him where he went, he said he had to smoke a cigarette. The sirens and whistles were going off inside of me.

When we pulled into his driveway, he really appeared excited for me to see his space. It was so beautiful I actually started crying. He had such a wonderful room and there was an in-ground, screened-in swimming pool/bar right outside his bedroom door. It really was a dream come true. Chris showed me how he set everything up in his space. "Like you do at home, Mom!" He expected me to take my shoes off at the door because he didn't want any sand in his space. I had to laugh out loud...laughed even harder when I saw the sweeper in the corner. He elaborated on why he picked out his colors, his bathroom cleaner, his scented candles, why he positioned his bed where he did, etc. etc. Sure sounded like my Chris, but my stomach was still bothering me.

I was telling myself over and over to knock it off and just have a good time. Chris spent long periods of time in the bathroom though. Of course I was suspicious. I learned to ask questions when I needed answers, but why did I expect him to suddenly tell the truth? As a parent I never gave up hope, which is a good thing. Chris said he was constipated. OK. Well, he had the same behaviors that I saw at home. His friend assured me that Chris was not doing drugs.

I was concerned at how quickly he would fall asleep sitting up with his head bobbing. I learned later it is called the "heroin bob." The fear was locking in. He adamantly denied relapsing. Another thing, he constantly sprayed his noise with Afrin. He said the allergies in Florida were really bad, explaining something about dead fish that washed up on shore and caused some type of fungus in the air to which he was allergic. OK.

Chris admitted that he lost his job at Naples Tomato because it was slow since it was summer. He was going to start a new job in a restaurant that was very busy all year. He felt bad that his first day was during my visit but I completely understood. The plan was for me to drop him off and use the car to shop around until he called for a ride home. No problem. I could shop until I dropped! He said he wasn't nervous about his new job but that's not how it appeared to me. He was sweating profusely and his nose was running constantly. He said it was allergies. OK. I was hoping it was first-day-on-the-job jitters but with the other symptoms I was seeing, I knew better. I drove away crying. I knew he was in trouble again and it was just going to be a matter of time before he would be back in rehab. I received a call from him in about twenty-five minutes. He was whispering in the phone for me to meet him next to a particular dumpster and to please stop and get him a bottle of Afrin because he couldn't breathe.

When I pulled up, he appeared to be hiding in the shadow of the dumpster on the side of the restaurant. He ran toward the car to get the Afrin. I watched him break the top off of it and pour it down his nose. My heart was racing and I started sobbing by this point. He waved for me to leave and I drove off. I sat in the parking lot sobbing. It was just about an hour later that he called for a ride home. He said his nose kept running and they told him to go home and that they would call in a few days. I knew what that meant. Again it was the same scenario, "Don't worry about me, Ma. I'm OK. I just don't feel good. It's my allergies."

I asked him to please go into treatment and he said he couldn't because he wasn't using. There really wasn't anything left to say. That night I couldn't sleep. I sat up most of the night watching him sleep on the floor next to the bed. He could hardly breathe during his sleep. I was watching someone who I could no longer help in life. He was a grown man that I feared was not going to make it. I prayed really hard that night. *God, please show him that you are here for him and guide him to some peace. Keep him strong in his faith and don't let anything happen to him. He wants to live and You know that more than anyone.*

I fell asleep for a short while and woke up on my birthday. *Happy birthday to me.* I hoped that my last full day with him would be different. He never mentioned his surprise and I knew not to ask. I didn't want to embarrass him. Something was trying to come through if you know what I mean. Divine intervention can be very strong and persistent for me. I'm sure it's like that for others as well. Something was telling me to go into the bathroom and look on the top shelf where Chris kept his towels. I know better than to ignore that type of intervention. It is intended for me. He was still snoring as I walked into the bathroom. I stood up on the toilet seat on my toes and reached my hand on the top shelf. I found a tissue. Whew, no big deal! *God, what is it? What do you want me to know?* I stepped down feeling very confused about the message and threw the tissue away. But the communication continued and it was stronger than ever. I was being told to run my fingers along the inside of the wood trim above that top shelf. I got back up there and did just that and immediately felt something round. It was a cardboard toilet paper roll. Inside the roll I found a bandana, a syringe and a spoon. I was too upset to look for anything more. I put the roll back where I found it and sat on the bed waiting for Chris to get up.

When he woke up he tried to get excited about my birthday. He said he had a card for me but never mentioned anything about a surprise. I knew if there once was one, he lost sight of it. He could tell I was bothered and he asked me what was wrong. I asked him if he had anything he wanted to tell me and of course he answered, "No, why?" I cried when I told him I found the drugs in the bathroom. He was shocked. "How did you know to look there?" He told me that his friends had ransacked his room looking for his drugs and never found any because they were so well hidden in that spot. We both were touched by how I knew to look there. I told him that God was trying to help in every way that He could but that Chris had to decide to help himself before it was too late. He agreed and said that he felt it was a divine intervention and he was going to take his life seriously. He cried and apologized to me again for hurting me and lying to me.

The day was very difficult even though we were touched spiritually so early in it. Chris had withdrawn and appeared ashamed. We went to a restaurant, but he didn't eat his meal. He fought with me instead. He was angry, saying I had no right to go through his things. My guess is he was going through withdrawal. He got up and left me sitting in the restaurant alone. I asked the waitress to box the food and when I walked outside, he was asleep on a chair on the porch. My heart was broken again. I really thought we turned the bend when he moved to Florida, but it was just more of the same. It was then that I realized that my son was very sick and that his disease could possibly kill him.

Late that afternoon, my office manager called me to tell me that a client of mine had an emergency and needed to talk to me. I had worked with her for a few years and knew that it had to be serious for her to call me on vacation. She was sobbing because her daughter overdosed on painkillers that morning and had died. It almost felt surreal with everything that was going on that week. I could feel the despair and fear building inside. I told Chris about the call because I was so upset. It seemed like God wanted him to know that his serious disease could kill, but everything continued to spiral downhill.

The next morning was equally as difficult. I had to catch my flight, but Chris was moving in slow motion. There wasn't any gas in the car and he didn't have any money to get more. We stopped to fill the tank and had to wait in line, which caused more delay. He was speeding to the airport and passed the exit. When I checked in late, they notified the pilot that I was there, so he wouldn't take off. He asked me not to leave but I couldn't stay. I couldn't help him anymore. I felt like I was slipping into a space out of which I was not going to be able to climb. I ran as fast as I could to catch my flight and didn't look back. That is one of the regrets I will always have in life. If I had stayed, would it have made a difference? I'll never know, but everything I had done to that point hadn't seemed to change our course. *Chris, I hope that you can forgive me for turning my back on you. I just couldn't help you at that point.*

I was sobbing by the time I boarded the plane. Everyone was strapped in their seats and I was aware that they were waiting for me and staring at me as tears streamed down my cheeks. The lady sitting next to me didn't even turn her head to look at me. I felt so alone and I wanted to scream out, *Stop the plane, I need to get off!* I didn't have the energy to do it. I really felt like I had a meltdown and needed to go home. All I could do was pray for my little love and turn him over to God. I knew all along Chris was in His hands, but wanted to believe that I had some sort of control over his destiny. "Stinking thinking" is what it's called in AA.

I was feeling very helpless and hopeless and anticipating a call from Chris about treatment. Sure enough, it came from his friend's mother a few weeks later. She was asked to let me know that Chris was in the Collier County Jail in Naples, Florida. He was picked up with two other friends. I was told that Chris had gone with two of his friends to buy cocaine. Apparently the house was under police surveillance. When they pulled away the police stopped them and searched the car. There was a small amount of cocaine in the middle console and the guy in the backseat had cocaine in his pocket. Due to the fact that no one claimed ownership of the cocaine in the console, the three of them were arrested and taken into custody. We were advised by the bondsman to not post bond since Chris had a previous felony conviction. The bondsman cautioned me that if he fled, there would be a warrant for his arrest and that could change the course of his life. He suggested that Chris remain in custody until the trial.

It was helpful to have Jay in the wings. From what the public defender told Jay, Chris was being charged with constructive possession of cocaine because he was in a car where it was found. They knew that it wasn't his, but it didn't change the charges. Florida is a zero-tolerance state.

So I dropped everything and my sister Cookie and I flew to Florida that weekend to pack, move and attend to the car as best we could. We had no idea what to expect once we got there, but assumed we would work out all of the details then. Storage was a big issue since it was hurricane season and there wasn't much available. There were a few wrenches in the formula: one was that I had broken my toe two days prior and my foot was black and blue and swollen. Two, my sister had a torn rotator cuff and was also in a lot of pain. We were really going to push ourselves to do the physical things that were necessary to pull this off in just three days.

Walking into the space where Chris lived was so incredibly sad for me. It was as though someone had died in there. Really, it was the death of our hopes of what life would be for Chris in Florida. His buddy had his things packed in boxes. I realize that it was a gesture of friendship, but it didn't feel that way to me. I felt like Chris's boundaries had been violated and I still wanted to protect him and the few things that he had left. I got over that quickly. There was much to do and no time for drama. We really struggled to get heavy boxes into the rental car and the storage unit. In the meantime we were making calls everywhere to find someone who would buy my father's car since we couldn't find a place to store it. The brakes were locked up and it couldn't be driven. In the middle of all of this, my foot was totally swollen, I couldn't walk without pain, my sister's shoulder was swollen and some sort of a spider or insect crawled in her sandal and bit her big toe. It was red and swollen. But oh no, that still wasn't enough drama. The temps were well into the high 90s or 100s. Our glasses were fogged up more than they weren't, we were sweating profusely, hungry, tired and, of course, scared.

That night we were permitted to see Chris for a twenty-minute visit. I was so angry with him that I decided on the drive over to Collier County Jail that I was not going in. All I wanted to do was walk away and never look back—until, of course, I was watching my sister walk into the facility without me. I honked for her to wait and I hobbled to the door with tears in my eyes, to see my little love. I loved him so much and couldn't even stay upset even when I knew it was in both of our best interests to do so. Tough love wasn't in my nature.

The experience was not what we expected. It was a lock-down facility and we could only talk to him through a television screen. They gave us fair warning that if he didn't hear his name called, we wouldn't be able to talk to him and could try again the next evening at the same time. We sat in front of a TV screen praying that he would hear his name. A few minutes later a door opened and all I could see were crutches coming through the doorway. There he was, dressed in the fashionable orange prison wear on crutches. He walked in front of the camera with a big smile because from where he was standing, he could see our sweaty tired pumpkin heads on the TV screen. As we typically did, we joked about everything. He said his foot was injured and started into detail, until we both told him to shut up because we were not only injured but we also had to carry his things into storage. We held our appendages in front of the camera so he could see the broken toe and spider bite. He was laughing so hard he had to wipe tears from his eyes. I wanted to grab his face through the camera and smack it ten times both ways, then maybe I would have felt like laughing too. But at that point I was just glad to see him. Twenty minutes felt like twenty seconds. In the middle of our conversation, the TV turned off and he was gone. My sister and I walked away with tears in our eyes and feeling very helpless but able to laugh about some of the funny parts. *Thank you, God, for bringing some light into our dark moments. How could I have made it without you?* I've said it many times before; when you need an angel they will usually appear. We had a beautiful condo to stay in that weekend on Marco Island, thanks to a family that generously offered it to us. Their son was going through the same thing and they were very supportive. Unfortunately their son passed away a month ago from drugs, another senseless death. *Thank you, Joe and Kathy. You were my angels when I needed one. I'm praying that you can find some comfort during this difficult time.*

Chris was upset that we had to move his things out of his space. He gave us a lead about the car. He said one of his friends wanted to buy it for $400 as is and asked us to follow up for him. "I'll need the money, Mom, when I get out of here. You can't just junk it, and it's a good car!" My sister and I were unsuccessful in trying to reach his co-worker. We were leaving the next day and were lucky enough to find a man who agreed to tow it to a junkyard. As the tow truck drove down the street with my dad's car on the back we watched the passenger car door fly open. I had flashbacks of my dad pulling up my driveway honking the horn with a cigarette hanging out of his mouth. My sister and I were silent watching the image of the car grow smaller and smaller. There was nothing to say; we both just silently cried.

Ma,

Ya I cant believe I've succomed this either. I am very disapointed in the way I've handled myself ever since day one that I've been down here in Florida. I am in aww that I've slipped back and regressed once again. As I sit in jail and think about everything, I think I am starting to second-guess my motives of why I really wanted to come down here, which is a very scary thing. I knew I relapsed even before I was off probation - I couldnt understand why either. I have not been in the right mental state ever since I started using, which is totally my fault. I think the reason is that I am not ready to grow up and move on - I constantly think about the past and how great it was and how everything was perfect before I started using. And night after night I've up praying and desprately searching for an answer - and some sort of reassurance that everythings going to be ok. I've come to see that everything in my life and I was most happy when I was not using, and that is where I truly need to be again in my life. I am such a good kid w/ the biggest heart you could ever imagine, but its just been steared in the wrong direction. I battle my addiction every day of my life because I do not do what I am suppose to do - I just sit and wait for something, a miracle if you may, to just happen to me and make it all better - but now I've come to realize that finally I'm sick and tired of bein sick and tired and the miracle needs to come from w/inside of me. And that is doing the right things, finally with my life. That means I have to give up and surrender - live a totally different life and totally change everything I've grown into the last 3 years. I need to reincarnate myself and really come to terms with what really matters in my life and the path I need to be on - I know you hear this from me alot when I relapse, but I truly think this time I'm gonna get it. I've never felt like this before ever since I started using. Maybe the miracle did happen - jail. This place has enabled me to really sit and evaluate my life and let me see the future and consequences first-hand of where I was going. I've never been here and I think I needed this, plus it allowed to become way more spiritual of myself and God. ~~I have gto~~ Let me explain something to you - you said I dont realize the severity of the situation I am in - You know, your absolutely right. I have become so "numb" to disapointments in my life that at first, actually the first week I was in jail, I didnt even care - I did not EVEN CARE. That is sick and degrading to me to think of the kid I once was, to what I am now that I do not even care that I am in JAIL?!!? How could I let my life slip like this and get to the point when I COULD CARE IF I WAS IN JAIL? I see a huge problem w/that, and the problem is me - my attitude and my outlook on life ever since I started using. ~~I've~~ I've

Come to a realization that everything in my life for the rest of my life is not going to be easy. I am ready to take this disease on first hand I think, for the first time since I started. Millions of people do it, so why cant I? I need to do the right things with my life which means no AJ, no drugs, no one from the past that uses, no more lieing, attend meeting gain a support group, get a non-using girlfriend, become holyer and surrender to God, pray and finally be the real Christopher Lee Burns that I once was. I was happiest when I wasnt using, and after the devil made his way to me, left his mark and now its time to grow up and end this non fruitful, terrible, sinned life I've been living. And I think jail, and the consequences of being here led me in the path finally where I need to be in - All my struggles and downfalls have come with a price, but mom please don't let that price ever be you giving up on me. You said your promise, well MY PROMISE TO ME AND YOU will be from now on, I will never be the selfish asshole that would have to put you in the predicament to rescue me, ever again. I vouch that from this day on, I will find my way and be the person whom I truly am at heart. Not this evil thing that I've turned into. I am so Thankful and everyday I pray and thank God that I have the family that I do, for my family is the absolutely only thing I have, and quite frankly I've come to learn that you guys are the only thing I need.

But from now on, I think I'm going to be ok, in fact what doesn't kill ya only makes you stronger - and with that said I must be the strongest idiotic dumbass in all the land. But thank you mom for standing by me, because I promise you it'll only get better from this point on — everything will be ok

love ya,
Chris

(a typewritten copy of this letter can be found in the Index page 121)

Ma,

Hey. I'm just sittin here here in jail in tears because of everything. I can't stand this shit anymore — Enough. It is not worth fu___ing my life up anymore than I already have. I have missed moments in my life that I will never be able to make up ever again. Every day in here feels like an eternity - for all I can do is sit and think and flash back my life. I can't stop thinking about the past and how much fun we all had and how great everything truly was. That was such a time of innocence. Remember the Halloweens we used to go on? And the Christmas caroling, and my big wheel, and rollerblade "Bauers", and go-kart, and hide and seek, and trip to Orlando with the E.T. ride, and muffins we ate every morning that were huge, and the Easter baskets you used to hide, and when you would pick me up every friday from school and we would go out to eat at China in the plaza, and trampoline, baseball, little Spartans, Maggie, and when Yvonne fell off the moped and her afro flew all over, and when you used to read us stories at night, and Jay used to wail every night. And remember the trips you would volunteer to go on with Miss Buffano, the Cleveland fairforest, Pittsburgh zoo, etc. I used to be so proud you were my mom, and every day that has passed I just keep realizing how proud and lucky I am to have you as my mom. I am missing so much of my youth b/c of this bullshit I keep doing to myself and its sad to say that jail really opened up my eyes and made me realize some really CRUCIAL things that I needed to see and realize - and I knew I can do it - and not for anybody but me. I think I live my life to try to please others avoiding the real problem, which I am slowly beginning to realize - I can do it. Millions of people do it, and are living a very fruitful life as a recovering addict - theres gonna be a lot of changes your gonna see in me from now on -

I sit here and think what I've lost and what I've done to myself and everybody and I am in pure awww that I could do things that I've done. I definitely have not lived the last 3 years honorably, and definitely not sinless. But ya know what mam? I have learned ALOT about myself, life, good, bad, and have knowledge beyond my years. I know God has a path for me that'll affect many lives, and I am so willing to get there. Just keep praying ma - because I know its working.

I love you -

Chris

Jay was working hard with the public defender to get Chris out of jail. Finally, he found a way. Less than six weeks later, Jay called me ecstatic that the case was being dismissed and Chris would be released that day. He said the public defender was going to personally walk the papers over to the jail. Jay felt that it would be a good idea if I purchased a one-way plane ticket for Chris to fly to California since he had no job and no place to stay in Florida.

"Mom, there's no problem with opiate addiction out here. People in Cali are pot smokers and cocaine users and he doesn't do either. It will be a good move for him and I will be able to watch over him. He'll love it out here."

I purchased a one-way ticket and he was off to California. I wired him some money which I found out later was used to buy an Oxy-Contin before he even left Florida.

He left everything of value in the storage unit and took a few suitcases of clothes with him. If any of your children have gone through this, you can probably relate to the amount of money wasted on things that you buy them to put a smile on their face. Later we all discover that their things are sold, traded, destroyed, stolen, etc. I wish I had the money today that I spent trying to make both of my children happy and comfortable wherever they lived. Randy told me MANY times that I was a horrible enabler and he is so right. But, I know in my heart that I did everything I could to create a home for them wherever they lived.

Anyhow, the move to California proved to be very positive. The boys were reunited and Jay showed Chris a little bit of heaven. Chris always wanted to live in the mountains.

When Jay first went to law school he lived in San Francisco. He really isn't a city dweller and when he could afford to move to a suburb, he did. He found a beautiful condo in San Rafael. Chris stayed with him and Jay's high school sweetheart Nicole.

Chris found a job quickly at the Outback where Nicole worked and he also found a job at Best Buy. He was working a lot, staying clean and enjoying life with Jay and Nicole.

A proud day for all of us: Jay's graduation from Golden Gate School of Law

He soon got a condo in the same complex where Jay and Nicole were living. It truly was a dream come true for me. Chris's condo had the most beautiful view of the mountains. He called it *heaven*. But as these sad stories go, it was only a matter of time before we were where we started out a few years before. Chris remained in denial and he didn't attend meetings or seek a sponsor. He was bright and without taking Adderall, he needed to find ways to stay stimulated. So it was a challenge for him to figure out how he could get around any system and break the rules. Once he found a way and began to make extra money, it was a trigger to use. Best Buy was his first challenge in California. As usual, he was promoted quickly, got bored and found ways to get fired.

Of course, he was beginning to regress in his behavior. Things were coming up missing at the apartment. Jay was having a hard time managing him with everything on his own plate. Chris got worse and needed to go through detox, so Jay made arrangements for it. Three days later, the hospital sent him home since he had to wait for a bed in a long-term treatment facility. In the three days that he waited for a bed, he relapsed but we didn't know that until later. Jay dropped him off at the treatment facility the beginning of the following week. He called me crying on the way home. This was taking a real toll on him. I was so concerned about Jay because the stress was affecting his job, his relationship with Nicole and his health. His blood pressure was really high and he was getting more and more depressed and less capable of keeping up with his own responsibilities. It was probably three hours later that Jay received the call that Chris would not be accepted into the program since he didn't pass the drug screen. Now what? We were back to feeling scared and trapped.

There were no other options but to send him home again. Jay and Nicole had gone as far as they could to try to help and I was checking into treatment programs in Ohio. The Teen Challenge was the only option. I knew that they had a history of being successful with other opiate addicts and at this point we felt grateful that they would accept him. He agreed to the program and he arrived back in Youngstown right before Christmas. As difficult as it was to put him in treatment at the holidays, we didn't really have a choice. Chris didn't argue or resist. He was compliant and quiet in the decision. He said this would be his last-ditch effort and he was going to live there as long as necessary in order to change his life. However, he was very concerned about the fact that he wasn't going to be able to smoke. He knew he could live without the drugs, but not the cigarettes.

Hope

Most of My Family, and others May see,
That I am down on bended knee –

Though my cheeks are drowning from the rain,
That doesnt even begin to tell my pain –

It seems ever since birth, so much I've gone through
But who the hell ever knew –

I was even born dyslexic,
but never I thought it would turn this hectic –

My life seems to be a constant battle,
I feel Im up the creek without a paddle –

But through it all I keep on trucking,
NEVER will I give up ducking –

1/9/07   11:15 am

Mom,
hey I just wanted you to see this real quick,
I keep writing these poems that keep coming
to me and they take me about 20 seconds to write.
I've written about 20 of them so far and have
thought of about 50 million in my mind

I wasn't as hopeful this time, maybe because Chris was fearful of not being able to smoke. I was even less hopeful when we moved him in there. I was not very impressed with the program and actually hated leaving him there. It was not at all what I thought it would be but I knew the alternative was death and so it had to be. I can go on and on about why I was uncomfortable with him being there, but we had exhausted all of our choices and with no medical insurance, we were lucky to find a program that would take him. Not to anyone's surprise, I received a call a few days later for me to pick him up because they caught him and several others smoking cigarettes. Chris begged them to let him stay because he was afraid that he was going to die if he was back out on the streets. When they caught him smoking a second time, they told me to pick him up or they were dropping him off at the nearby bus station.

There were no more places to go. He appeared stable when my sister and I picked him up that night. He was making plans to return to California after Jay took his bar exam in February. Jay couldn't handle the stress of Chris being there during that time, which was understandable. During those couple of weeks he relapsed and I saw more of the same - nervousness, missing things around the house, etc. The drug dealers were coming to the house doing deals with him in the drive. I found syringes on the dresser when I cleaned it. I was fearful at times for my own life and his. It reached the point that I thought it never would. I broke. I told him that he had to stay in our local rescue mission and he agreed to go. We had been on the phone trying desperately to get him admitted to some of the local treatment facilities but we didn't get a call back from any of them. That was another eye-opener for me.

I asked my sister to drive him to the mission but instead she offered to have him stay at her apartment for three weeks before his flight to California. It was as though Jay and I were taking turns caring for him and had to give each other a break every few months or so. It was truly a crazy life. We were a mess as a family. I really don't know how either one of us got through it, but we did. My faith kept me strong during the darkest moments. It was all I had. I still don't know what Jay did to get by. Before Chris left that afternoon to stay at my sister's, he asked for money and I went after him with my boot. I hit him on his back and his arm. He thought I lost my mind because it was so out of character for me. I screamed at him and told him that I hated him and he just let me go on and on. I guess it was what I needed to do. I had my first and only meltdown that day. He gathered his things and when he went out the door he looked over at me with a smile. I'll never forget what he said. *"Ma, I'm so proud of you. You needed to do that a long time ago. It's about time. I'm so sorry that I got you to this point but I'm so glad you said what you needed to say. I love you, Ma."* And he left. It seemed to be a very cathartic moment for us. My sister said he got in the car and was rubbing his arm and they both busted out laughing.... always something to laugh about. Before I knew it, the weeks passed and we were driving to the airport. He had no money, no plans for a future, but a little excitement about a girl that Nicole was fixing him up with, an ex-heroin addict. He loaded her picture as his screen saver and thought his new life would include her.

"It's going to be different, Ma. I don't have anything left now...no pride even. I'm going to go to meetings with her and finally change my life."

From everything I've learned about drug addiction, some of the damaged brain cells can never be repaired. There is something to be said for that. As Chris continued to use, I knew that he was causing damage to his brain. His thinking became very irrational, his ability to reason and remember deteriorated. His connection to me was fading. I saw it in his eyes. When he talked about his life before drugs, I could always see joy in his eyes. He would display signs of excitement, meaning, fear, sadness, glee; you name it, you could feel it and see it in him. That's what made him so unique. As he would share his experiences, it was easy to relate.

In looking back on his fall into addiction, I grew to be very intuitive. That is one of the blessings of living with someone suffering from addiction. It is most helpful to stay calm before reacting. When a parent discovers that their child is using a deadly drug, the shock and trauma can create a disorder called PTSD (post traumatic stress disorder). There are several symptoms of PTSD and for most sufferers, hyper vigilance and hypersensitivity to detail, is very disturbing. It can create relives and reenactments of the actual trauma. When experiencing PTSD, our sensory pathways do not screen or filter as they should. Consequently, what we see, hear, taste, touch and smell can exacerbate the symptoms of PTSD. This can lead to a vicious cycle.

Any sufferer of PTSD will need to learn to control the symptoms of it, to avoid additional trauma. If you are suffering from PTSD, it is helpful to get evaluated for an antidepressant and pursue therapy, which will help to treat the debilitating symptoms. I found the amino acid, 5-HTP very helpful for my symptoms of PTSD. It helps to quiet the mind, reduce anxiety and taken at bed, it will induce sleep. It's a wonderful supplement that can be purchased in a health food store.

PTSD was triggered often for me. It began for me when I saw the needle marks on his arms. From that point, if it was triggered, I would quickly draw conclusions that would create unnecessary stress for me. A good example is when something turned up "missing". I would assume that Chris stole it for drug money. My PTSD would flare up, once I calmed down, my intuition would give me a lead to find it. Often I would. In the meantime, Chris and I would argue and I wouldn't believe a word he said, which creates more drama. There were times, I couldn't help myself and we would have to dig out of the mess that PTSD created.

My rule of thumb is to ignore intrusive thoughts which can be very negative. I do that by repeating to myself, *it is only a thought, it isn't real*. With practice, this can prevent the emotional reaction that a disturbing thought can create. Also, it gives a parent an opportunity to gather the facts. My mantra is...*it isn't a problem until it's a problem, and God will not give me something I cannot handle.*

As parents we must accept that there will be consequences to living a life with an addicted child and PTSD is one. Don't expect your child to understand or be supportive of what you are going through. It is ultimately our responsibility to keep ourselves healthy and it is critical that we try during these difficult times in life.

There aren't many things that I would do differently, but one would be to attend Al-Anon meetings more often. I've been counseling others for over thirty years and it was difficult for me to step out of my role when I would attend a meeting, to get the help I needed for myself. There were times when I walked in and saw two or more of my clients sitting in the meetings. I started my own support group which eventually fizzled out.

As the addiction was killing his spirit and brain, he didn't have that connection with life any longer. I attempted to rekindle it for him by sharing things about the people he loved; something funny about Ginger or something upsetting that happened to one of us. But Chris wasn't there. He was no longer in the moment where he existed with such passion. I couldn't find him when I looked into his eyes and I knew he was dying. What I once had, I would never have again. We begin to let go of this life when we are getting prepared and closer to leaving it. I feel strongly that Chris was in that part of the journey and it kept me in a constant state of terror and fear. Parents who go through this know what I'm talking about. We wait for that call to come and on some level we are aware that it's coming. When I received that call from Jay on April 19, 2007, I knew it was THAT call. I sobbed before I even returned it and I had gotten so many of those calls and never had that reaction.

I typed out the last text messages that I received from him. He regressed quickly when he returned to California. I tried to keep in touch with him every day but he wasn't returning my calls or even my texts. I knew we were getting closer to something very devastating. I was in constant fear and couldn't sleep or concentrate. I was having nightmares of Chris dying; being chased, beaten up, tortured…it was a very difficult time for me. I was up through the night asking God to give me the strength for what was coming. A Christian friend of mine, gave me the *Prayer of Jabez* and it was so helpful for me during this time. I continue to say the prayer daily.

I felt strongly that my path was being paved for something very grand on a spiritual level and I was right. I've known all along that I came to the Earth to serve God. I believe that I must follow my heart and not my pain to be able to use my experiences to grow. I am so humbled by the lessons that have been given to me in my lifetime. They are not a mistake, they are necessary for me to understand who I am and my relationship with God.

Thursday, March 29 @ 5:56 p.m.
Thanks for the blessing. This is beyond drugs, mom, I'm screwed up and I don't know if I will recover and be myself again but either way this is my final stop.

Thursday March 29th @ 6:00 p.m.
This is the last straw for me. I know that im scared if it doesn't work 4 me I wont be able to pick myself back up again. I lost my passion and goals and self worth

Thursday March 29 @ 6:06 p.m.
I'm goin in as the underdog and have one last stand left before I'm totally gone and call it a day. Just keep prayin I need all the help I can get

Friday April 6th @ 11:52 a.m.
I lucked out 2day and landed an interview

Sunday April 15th @ 9:37 p.m.
Thank you mom for calling me, u put the first smile on my face in days, please just at least call me, it makes a huge difference 4 me 2 know u still care

That was the last time I heard from Chris. His spirit was broken. He had given up his battle. Jay received the call from the police on the morning of the 19. The girl he was dating, the one who was in the motel with him that night, reported the events from the night that he died to the police. She said they were using and she passed out. She told us that she awoke to him gasping for air. She placed a towel under his neck to help him breathe and fell back to sleep. In the morning she found him dead. The police did not feel there was a need to further the investigation but we disagreed. Mainly because there were drugs in him that Jay swore he never took and the other reason was that he was going to receive a check from Social Security. We suspected foul play after she told us that Chris wanted her to have this money if something happened to him. We didn't have a clue what she was talking about and it wasn't the time to get distracted on other issues. Later it was confirmed through Social Security that he was in fact going to receive checks monthly for a year. The gentleman I spoke with remembered Chris and said he appeared very confused when he was explaining how California disperses monies. Chris either misunderstood or lied to her to keep her near since he wasn't well and fearful of being alone. That will forever remain a mystery with us.

Chris was so simple that it made him beautiful. He loved backpacks. When his body was picked up at the motel, his backpack was in the room. He had a toothbrush, comb, pack of gum, a picture of the three of us, a mini book that Jay had bought him about brothers and a small note that Jay had written to him when he left for college and a set of black rosary beads. Those had to be his "treasures," a word he often used as a small child. He was forever taking pictures, but we never found his camera.

I believe his spirit was dying during his last few months on the Earth. By the time his brain had died, his memory of what he was and what he wanted to become was out of his reach. It is so painful to think about. How could this have happened to such a beautiful soul so full of joy and so interested in living life? What he referred to as his *demon* had won. Deep in my heart I believe his soul is with God and it lives again with a renewed and restored spirit, somewhere over the rainbow.

MEMORIES... CHRIS'S FOOTPRINTS ON OUR HEARTS

Chris took his last breath at around 5:30 a.m. on April 24, 2007 and life changed forever. I've chosen to believe that when we die our soul reunites with God and we get an opportunity to quickly rewind through our lifetime so that we can see what lessons we learned. That is how we understand how one dot connects to the other. I wonder what all of the dots meant for Chris and what my dot that connected to him will mean yet. I wouldn't have discovered my beliefs, my relationship with my angels and my God if those dots hadn't connected the way they did.

I read once that, "People will forget what you said. People will forget what you did. But, people will NEVER forget how you made them feel." Chris helped many of us reach into the depths of our souls in order to survive the fear and pain that his addiction created during the years that he was ill. But he also brought us to the epitome of joy, happiness, laughter and love. He touched many people, young and old.

Chris lived a more meaningful life in twenty-three years than most of us do in a full lifetime. How can that be? He lived simply, he found the joy and laughter in the moment, and he sat on Mt. Tam, Starbucks in hand, one with nature, and one with God.

Chris had a huge heart. Everyone he came across fell in love with him.
(Taken from the eulogy written by Cousin Heather)

I feel that his story cannot end without sharing some of the comments and gestures that others have made in honor of his life on Earth. He left his "footprints" on our hearts.

Christopher Burns
"Remember the joy, the laughter, the smile.
I've only gone to rest a little while."

Stephanie, Chris's high school sweetheart, wanted to do something special for Chris. She posted her desire to dedicate a park bench in honor of him, on his MySpace page, which Jay maintains as a memorial to remember Chris as the beautiful person he was at **www.myspace.com/burnz2**. She was able to raise enough money and the bench sits by a stream at the half-mile marker on the three-mile mile bike/walk trail in Boardman, OH. The tired walkers and runners in the park have a beautiful place to rest.

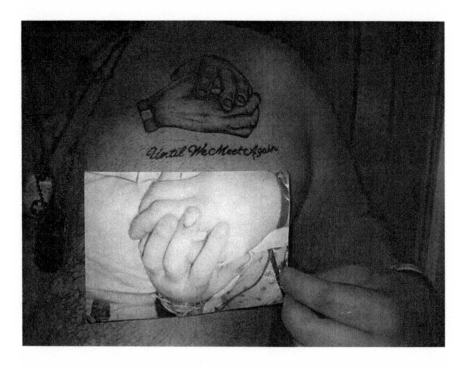

Jay asked the nurses to place Chris's hands in the prayer pose moments before they took him off life support. He had Debbie Lenz, from Artistic Dermagraphics in Boardman, Ohio, tattoo it on his chest one week after Chris passed away.

THANKSGIVING 2007

A story of loss and hope

Mother honors her late son by helping others

By AMANDA C. DAVIS
VINDICATOR CORRESPONDENT

"Thank you mom for calling me, u put the first smile on my face in days. Please just at least call me, it makes a huge difference 4 me 2 know u still care."

This is the last time Marilyn Burns heard from her 23-year-old son, Chris, when he sent her a text message at 9:37 p.m. on Sunday, April 15.

Within a few days, he would be laying in a hospital outside San Rafael, Ca., hooked up to life support after suffering a drug-related heart attack.

The text message, which she saved, was in response to one she sent earlier in the week, urging him to hang in there and reminding him that she loved him. She knew he was in trouble.

Chris' story is one that chronicles the pain and desperation of addiction, the ups and downs of recovery and the spiritual journey of a family, trying to make sense of a young life cut short.

Chris was born June 17, 1983, to Marilyn and Randy Burns of Boardman.

Thanksgiving was always Chris' favorite holiday, Marilyn said, explaining she knew she had to spend that day doing something meaningful to honor him.

She settled on serving meals at Youngstown's Rescue Mission, along with her brother, Don Arditi of Columbus.

As a mental health counselor and director of Canfield's Treat Yourself Center for Holistic Health, Marilyn has experience treating people with neurological impairments, drug problems and a host of other issues. This helped her to deal with Chris when he was born with Attention Deficit Disorder and dyslexia, and later when he became addicted.

She said his disorder gave Chris a greater sense of empathy and compassion for others.

From the beginning, Marilyn said she knew her son was special.

"I always felt he was an angel on this earth for a reason," she said. "Down deep inside, there was something so pure about him — his heart was huge."

Chris graduated from Boardman High

See Hope on Page A4

The Vindicator/William D. Lewis

A MOTHER GRIEVES: Marilyn Burns of Boardman looks at a photograph of her son Chris, 23, who died in April after suffering a heart attack caused by drug use. Burns spent Thanksgiving serving meals at the Rescue Mission in Youngstown as a meaningful way to remember her son, whose favorite holiday was Thanksgiving. Chris Burns' problems with drugs started in 2002 after he was in a car accident that left him with a broken back and other injuries and he was introduced to the powerful painkiller OxyContin.

99

HOPE

Continued from A1

School in 2002, where he had played football. That summer, before he was to leave for Mount Union College, he was in a car accident that left him with a broken back and other injuries.

He started his freshman year and was in chronic pain when someone turned him onto OxyContin, a powerful painkiller that gives users a heroinlike high. From there, things went downhill and Chris ended up twice at Glenbeigh's rehab facility in Rock Creek.

After the second stay, Marilyn said Chris moved to Naples, Fla., to stay with friends from the Youngstown area and look for work. Doing well and making good money at a restaurant there, Marilyn thought Chris had turned the corner.

Then she decided to visit in May 2004, a combined Mother's Day and birthday present for herself. "I knew he was in trouble again the minute I stepped off the plane," she said. "His eyes didn't look right and he was nervous."

After a sleepless night, Marilyn said a great sense of intuition compelled her to check a shelf in his bathroom. Behind it is where she found drug paraphernalia.

In that moment, Marilyn was both mortified for her son and humbled by what she said was a higher power that led her to the truth. She waited until he awoke and confronted him with what she found. This time he had to get clean for good, she told him.

Marilyn said Chris' brother Jason was living in San Rafael, Ca., and wanted Chris to move out there in late 2004 and start over. He did OK for awhile, she said, but eventually found his way back to drugs.

He returned to Boardman a few days after Thanksgiving last year and entered rehab in the Teen Challenge program in Cleveland. He was kicked out in February for smoking cigarettes and headed back to California, vowing to get help there.

Still in pain, Chris finally went to a doctor who put him on Prozac and methadone to help wean him off whatever opiates he was taking. He also agreed to start physical therapy again.

About a week before his heart attack, Marilyn said she had a dream of him in a coffin.

"I couldn't sleep; I couldn't breathe," she explained. "I called him and warned him and he got scared."

He promised to get it together, told her he was going to finish school to become a counselor and that he eventually wanted to take over her practice so he could help others.

Chris was staying at a hotel with a girlfriend and wasn't returning calls from his mother or brother. That's when he had the heart attack, after mixing a combination of prescribed drugs — including methadone, Prozac and Adderall — and opiates which he had not been prescribed.

He was brain dead and on life support by the time Marilyn and Chris' father flew out there.

Doctors said he would never recover and Marilyn said she initially fought that idea. She wanted a second opinion and more tests, but needed time to think.

While resting in the hospital, she said she must have dozed off.

"I had a dream and he came to me as clear as could be and said, 'Let me go, Mom. I'm already gone.'" He was taken off life support, transported back to Youngstown and buried a few days later in Calvary Cemetery.

This time of year is especially hard for both Marilyn and Jason as they continue to struggle with the loss. "I've made it seven months now and I'm thankful I had him for 23 years because he brought me huge joy," she said.

Jason, 26, still lives in San Rafael where he works at a law firm while waiting to take the bar exam. He said his feelings about his brother's death can best be summed up by the word he got tattooed on his forearm shortly after — "Broken."

While Chris lay in the hospital, Marilyn positioned his hands as if he were praying and took a picture. That picture was taken to Artistic Dermagraphics in Boardman where owner Debbie Lenz turned it into a tattoo over Jason's heart. Below it

appear the words "Until we meet again."

Marilyn said she still feels Chris around her and often talks to him, taking comfort in the fact that he's now safe.

Her advice for others dealing with addicts is to never shut them out. "You don't have to excuse their behavior or enable them," she said. "Just tell them you love them; I said what I had to say and I have no regrets or loose ends."

Chris' unpacked suitcase that came back from California still sits in his bedroom at his mother's house. A rosary hangs on the outside of his door and several more lay on a night stand and dresser. His mom said his faith and church were both extremely important to him.

There are also letters and poems he wrote, chronicling his thoughts, hope and at times, despair.

He knew his pain had a higher purpose — for his story to help others — and to get it out there. Marilyn plans to soon write a book about him.

"It didn't matter how sick Chris got, even in the darkest part of his addiction, he kept saying that God had a plan for him," Marilyn said.

He eluded to that in a letter he sent his mother while trying to stay clean in Florida.

"I know God has a path for me that'll affect many lives, and I am so willing to get there. Just keep praying ma — because I know it's working. I love you — Chris."

The Youngstown Vindicator did a feature story on us during the first holiday season after Chris died. I received two calls from parents who were going through the same thing. They said it gave them hope and I know that is exactly what Chris would have wanted. Amanda Davis, who also edited this manuscript, wrote the article.

I owned a holistic health center at the time that Chris died. As part of many services offered, was the drum circle that met there weekly. I was touched when the drum circle gathered donations to plant a tree at the Villa Maria Retreat Center in Pennsylvania in honor of Chris' life on Earth. He made it known to everyone how much he loved nature. This fruit tree will someday bear fruit to help feed the many people that the Villa Maria serves every day. The sisters of the Humility of Mary order donate the organic fruits and veggies to our local food banks from what they harvest from their land.

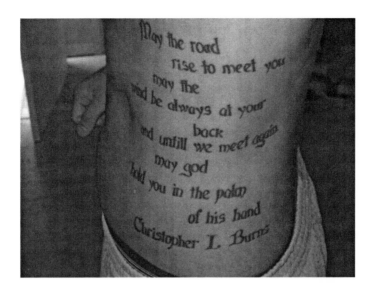

My nephew Tommy was devastated when Chris died. They had planned to live together in Cali, but it was not in the divine plan. In honor of him, he had one of Chris' favorite sayings tattooed on his side...the Irish Blessing.

Excerpts from www.myspace.com/burnz2, from his brother Jay

July 10, 2007...Hey Lil bro. I just wanted to stop by and tell you how much I miss you. For some reason it has been really hard for me lately. It is almost like the more time that passes, the worse I get with the grief over losing my best friend and little brother. Chris, I swear, I would give anything to go back and do things differently. I am so sorry if I failed you as an older brother. I tried so hard to do the best that I could to help and guide you through the years, I hope that you know that I would have given up my life if it would have saved yours. In fact, I think that it is almost unfair that I am still here and you are gone, as you had such an amazing drive to live life with a smile on your face no matter how broken you were on the inside. You tried so hard to beat your addiction and through all the hardships you faced since you were young, you never lost faith or gave up. You are so strong Bro, way stronger than me, and taller (see I finally gave you props), and I wish I had just a little bit of those traits in me, because maybe it would help me get though this all. I love you so very much Chris, I just wanted to tell you that because I know that you check this site daily, just as you did when you were on my couch. I just hope that people do not forget you because I know that I wont and never ever will. I hold you right next to my heart, literally, hence the tat I got of your hands. I am thinking about you now and always and miss and love you more and more every day that you are not here. I cannot wait until we are together again, as then, I will feel alive again, because I will be reunited with my other half. I love you Lil bra. Good night.

June 17, 2007 12:00 am Happy birthday to you, happy birthday to you, happy birthday little Bro, happy birthday to you. You have to blow out your candles now....as you can see, the "2" candle is on your double cheeseburger from Mcd's and the "4" is on the Swiss cake little Debbie. Just how you loved it-dinner and desert. I hope you don't get too mad because I would not want it to go to waste, so I'm going to house it. Chris, tonight, the eve of your birthday, Nikki and I went to the lake up in the mountains that me and you discovered. Yes, the same place we caught the baby rattler snake and you put it in your sock and we kept it as a "pet" and got reamed by Ma (LOL). I got you a Happy Birthday balloon; we talked to you and let it go. As it continued to rise up into the sky, I felt as if you were there watching over us, wiping our tears, waiting for the balloon to get to you and I felt as if we were moving closer together. Then, as Nikki noticed, that huge bright star appeared and it was not even dark yet. I know that was you Chris. I see you up there every single night watching over me when I get home from work. You are so far away though...I just want to reach out and touch your hand and face and tell you how much I love you and how badly I miss you and how I would give my whole life away just to be able to do that. Something that people take for granted, like picking up your phone to call your loved one, or NEVER ending a night in an argument, because you never know if you will have the next morning to make up. So, to all, on my little brother's 24th birthday, please do not take your loved ones for granted. I would do anything and everything to do those simple things with Chris again, but I will never be able to do so. Do not be too proud to apologize even if you were not in the wrong because you never know when it will be too late. I love and miss you Chris, more than anything. Happy Birthday little Bro. Until we meet again.....your big Bro.

June 4, 2007 What's up little Bro? Well it has been 41 days since you left this world and it still feels like it was yesterday. The daily pain and anguish is still unbearable. Man, I still break down at least once a day, if not more. I just cannot imagine doing this for the rest of my life. People keep telling me that it is going to get easier with time. Well, while for most people that is the anecdote, for me, it is not happening. I miss you so much Chris. I have never wanted anything more than to have you back here with me. You are everything to me and now that you are gone my heart is broken, with no chance of mending it. Last weekend I went to that lake up in the mountains behind College of Marin we discovered a few weeks before you passed away. I brought an extra chair for you and the pole I bought you that you never even got to take out of the package. It is times like those that I miss you the most. The times that we cherished so much. Just me, you, a net, a couple fishing poles, and a container for whatever critter I happened to catch on our weekly journeys. Every morning I wake up and on my daily trek to the kitchen to eat whatever little Debbie product we have left, I still picture you sleeping on that couch. Every night after working my 12 hour days, I look down at my cell hoping to see "Lil Bro" under my missed calls, or see your text messages telling me to leave work and come home to play Madden with you. My life is so empty and hollow without you here Chris, I cannot stand it. My life will never be the same little Bro, but I hope that you hear this plea to guide and help me right now because I need you so badly to provide me with the strength and perseverance to get through this, not even to get me back to how it was before this tremendous tragedy, but to show me that there is a purpose for me to remain here and not be back together with you again, the way it should be. I cannot do it alone and I have proven that by writing this message to you. I love you so much Chris and there is not one second that goes by that I do not wish you were here with me again. I love you more than words can say. Your broken big Bro.

Chris I still don't believe this is true...seems like a bad dream. (www.myspace.com/burnz2)

Euology written for Chris by his brother Jay

What is it that we remember when we think of my little Brother Chris? I think everyone who knows him would agree with me on this. It was his sense of humor, his uncanny ability to make us smile no matter the situation and last but not least his huge heart. He was the kind of person that would make everyone laugh so hard that they'd end up crying, even if you were mad at him. That is what I will truly miss about Chris. He always cheered me up when he knew I just had a bad day, which occurs more than one would think. That's the trademark of a Brother, my Brother. He always wanted to make people happy and would do so at any expense.

Chris's death was sudden. I remember when Nikki and myself heard the news we simply could not believe it. The thoughts of not having my little Brother were running through my head like a freight train. We completely panicked, as at the time, I could not even imagine not being able to pick up the phone a few....hundred times a day and talk to him or play Madden with him 6 times every night. My little Bro was too young but over the past few days I have realized that Chris indeed lived his life wonderfully and how he wanted to live it. He was well-loved and he had accomplished so many things on Earth and I'm sure he'll do much more in heaven watching down on all of us.

While on Earth he was unable to do what he wanted so badly, which was to help others fight their battle with addiction. The kid was barely hanging on, but in talking to him, you would never know it. That is because he had that unique personality trait, the ability to mask his pain, enabling him to keep on truckin, determined to make his mark on this world and to be remembered, not for little things he did wrong, but for all he did right. Chris. You knew that I would have given my life for you to be well again. If I could have taken every ounce of pain from you and put it on me, I would have. I would have done anything for you, no questions asked. I will never have another Brother, nor will I ever be able to fill that enormous void in my heart that solely belongs to you. I will however be able to close my eyes and picture you in Heaven, completely well and painless, free of the daily restrictions and burdens.

Therefore, I know that God is a better man and Brother than I could ever be to you in that respect. He gave you the greatest gift of all, which is freedom, and for that, I will be forever thankful. I am also thankful that I have so many wonderful memories of you and I over the past 23 years. So much of my Brother is in me—we are so similar—that perhaps the best tribute I can give—the best way for me to keep his spirit alive—is to honor and express all his positive qualities in me and live in a way that would continue his essence and make him proud.

My mother told me a couple nights ago that once Chris was taken off life support she was breathing for him and when she feels like the pain is so unbearable she asks him to breathe for her, he answers her prayer. Well little Bro, I need you now, more than anyone will ever know or can imagine. I think of all the seconds, minutes, hours, days and years left in my life and all the new memories that time will consist of and the thought of not having you to share it with deeply saddens me. You know that you were my world and while you did look up to me, I looked up to you as well. You were strong and I admired you for that. Your determination and perseverance was, and will forever be, unprecedented.

See Chris, you thought you were alone on this Earth, with just a handful of people who cared about you. Let me be the first to tell you that you could have never been so mistaken. The hardest thing that I ever had to do was stand there yesterday and watch the hundreds of people walk through that funeral home and pay their respects to you. Many shared with me how special you were to them and how you touched their lives in such a special way. I watched your best friend try and say goodbye to you, as the tears rolled down his face. I saw a girl who you shared a special love with attempt to make her peace with you and ask you for the strength to make it through this difficult time.

May the road rise to meet you, May the wind be always at your back, May the sun shine warm upon your face, The rains fall soft upon your fields and, Until we meet again, May God hold you in the palm of His hand.

A wonderful man filled our hearts, but now is gone...and there is a hole left in the world... Chris will forever live in my heart... In our hearts. Rest in Peace little Bro. I love you so much and miss you terribly. Until we meet again...

INSIGHT

> Life will never be complete without Chris but I know heaven is now complete because he is now home. (Taken from the eulogy written by Cousin Heather)

Lost No More is about opening your mind and your heart to a belief system that will serve you well through life and change the meaning of your experiences. I've read many times that as one door closes another one opens. I've had to close the door to my mind that I lost a son and open the door to believing that he is still with me and I can still have a relationship with him...but on a much deeper level. How can I say that with such confidence and certainty??? Because I finally woke up from ...living in the dark about death. I've spent many nights crying myself to sleep since my son died and what I have learned from those sleepless nights is this:

When I asked God...*why did you do this...why did you take Chris from me.*...I was so surprised at what came to me, in fact, it brought me to tears. What I heard was *why not... you are worthy of growing spiritually, it's your time.* I remembered the Prayer of Jabez and the message in the prayer nestled in a place within me where my deeper sense of knowing exists. I replay that message often…*why not, it's your time.*

First of all, I've come to accept that I was lead to be a therapist on this Earth. It is what I do and after thirty-one years of practicing, I can still do it with ease and effectively. There were many times in my sessions that I channeled information that came to me, not realizing it until many years later. **That** information—a word, a phrase, a question, a thought, a suggestion, etc.—would relieve my client's pain and suffering. I LEARNED to trust God's path for me….how? Because the insights that came to me I confidently shared….and it HELPED.

Back in the 70s and 80s as an unseasoned therapist, I wondered why God allowed so many of my precious clients to experience such horrific things in life. I wondered if there was even a God. Forgive me for doubting Him but it was all part of a process for me. What I've learned to accept is that it is through our darkest moments in life that we somehow find our way to Him. God gives us a few helpful tools to help us on this journey: free will and prayer to name a few. How brilliant He is!! Those who have found their way to prayer have been on the path to survive a child's death without even knowing it. I know, I know…this sounds crazy…but I get so excited when God allows me to help…AND WHEN it WORKS!! So I'm asking you to trust what I am saying and try to keep your mind and your heart open for a few more minutes. Most of us have found our way to a dark moment/time in life. Why? Because we HAVE to. It's the pathway to spiritual growth and awareness.

Once we discover the power of prayer, we can find an answer or solution to our WHY. Think about it: we trust that God is guiding us; we talk to God all the time; we imagine how God is working miracles for us. We KNOW it to be true, so why are so many people still suffering??? They say they trust; they say they know that God is working for them, but they aren't allowing those beliefs to work. **They refuse to let their faith work for them; they won't TRUST, let go.....and see what happens next**!!! It's pretty incredible when you can do that!

Once you have lost a child, you have to find a way to get relief from that grief or you won't make it, literally. You will die a spiritual death; I've seen it in my practice. God has given us prayer, which is a spiritual way of talking to Him as a way of getting relief. Why wouldn't it work for us when we lose someone that we love???? We can still talk to them. We continue to cry with them, laugh with them, love and live life with them...in the same **traditional way that God taught us to have a relationship with Him! He gave us the tools to survive our tragedies without us even realizing it. He gives us free will to decide what we want to believe. Why not believe in something that can help to heal emotional pain. God was a genius to give us the tool of prayer. He is a very loving and steadfast parent. We have the best, don't we???**

The moment I received that call from Jay, I began to have the relationship with Chris as I live it today. It is as real as the one I had with him for twenty-three years. It makes me smile, makes me laugh, makes me cry and I continue to grow through it. It is more powerful every day because it is on the same level as my relationship with God or my higher power.

I have learned to trust the way in which Chris communicates with me today. A good example is the process I went through to write this manuscript. He communicated often during my sleep when he wanted me to put something in the manuscript or to change it somehow. Two weeks ago I was very comfortable with the cover. I asked several people for their opinions and I sketched my final draft. Jay and I agreed that it was great. Last week during the night I woke out of a deep sleep with the clear image of what Chris wanted for the cover. After the editor suggested a change, special consideration was given and I decided to change it just recently.

One of my clients made a comment about the change in the cover *sometimes we don't get what we want in life or in death!* She made me laugh with that comment.

I usually don't remember my dreams and so he has to wake me out of a deep sleep to let me know what he wants. Since it happened so often in the beginning, I purchased a small recorder. When I would wake up with ideas, phrases, etc. I just recorded them so I could get back to sleep. I think he is still ADHD!! I've had so many sleepless nights during the writing of this manuscript; I purchased a sleep-aid spray called Rescue Remedy Sleep Spray. He would wake me with something he felt was important, I would record it, spray Rescue Remedy Sleep Spray, eventually fall back to sleep. And then, he would wake me when he thought of something else. I would record, spray, fall back…unbelievable. Some things I guess will never change! The night he wanted me to change the cover he woke me three times and then I got mad and told him if he woke me one more time, he was going to have to finish the book himself! I slept the rest of the night. You might ask how I know it was Chris; I don't, but I'm choosing to believe it.

Our relationship with God is spiritual, it is real and it has always been a meaningful way for us to communicate with Him. We need to acknowledge and accept that it really is a form of communication. It is the first form of communication that we have with our children. When that ob-gyn tells us that we are pregnant, it **begins** then. We start talking to our child and sharing life with them without ever seeing them or holding them or knowing who they are. That is when we begin to love them and change through our love for them. And I believe that they love us back on a soul level. It is profound; it is powerful; and it is God's way. Our children are the angels that God sends our way to help us **grow up spiritually**. How magnificent is that??? And to think we are socialized to believe that we are put here to help **them** grow up…hmmmm….a little twist of fate.

June 2002 written for his graduation from Boardman High School:

Dear Chris,

June 17, 1983 was a day I'll never forget. How scared I was to go to the hospital because the doctors told me that there could possibly be something wrong with you...and the doctors were right, there was something different...**you were born an angel**. Tearfully, I counted every toe and finger...two eyes, a nose and strong arms and legs to carry you through life. Whew was I relieved! God knows, that those legs never stopped moving and that mouth never stopped talking! But **your smile**, Chris, it warmed every heart that saw it..especially mine.

I want to thank you for teaching me about life in ways that I could never have hoped or imagined. You taught me never to give up. Every time I watched you trying so hard to sound out words, write your name, learn to ride your bike, or throw a ball..I knew that I would survive raising you and Jay! Only God knows how difficult that has been for me!

You taught me to see life through it's differences...we know that not everyone is alike. You learned differently and so my life was different because of you. Your sensitivities, strength, courage and determination taught me that the challenges in life are not walls, but just bridges to get us exactly where we need to be. You showed me how to get there. I watched you do it. And therefore I could. And now, here you are, off to Mount Union ready to cross another bridge to get to where you want to be. How proud I am of you, Chris.

I watched you grow into the loving, caring, fun, attentive man that you are.
You are a true inspiration for **all** men. When God gave you to me, I never realized the magnitude of the gift I would be given. Watching you grow has been such a joy for me...one of the most joyful experiences of my life.

It is time for you to move on and for me to remember everything that you have taught me...as I have to face my life alone after all of these years. Wherever you go in life, Chris, just know that there won't be a day in your life that I won't be thinking of you and praying that you will finally be living the life that you deserve. I can't thank you enough for being the "wind beneath my wings" on those days when I wasn't sure if I had the strength to keep on going...your warmth and smile always helped.

I hope that God will allow me to grow old with you because I can't imagine my life any other way. You are the most wonderful person I know in life...and how lucky I was that God picked me to be your mother. **That's how I know there is a God in my life...he sent me an angel, when he gave you to me.**

Thank you sweetheart, for all of the wonderful, tender memories that I will always carry in my heart. I am going to miss you more than you will ever know. I am your #1 fan...so you go and make your life the BEST THAT IT CAN BE AND DON'T EVER EVER FORGET WHO YOU ARE...YOU ARE A BEAUTIFUL MAN ...INSIDE...AND OUT.
I'LL LOVE YOU FOREVER AND ALWAYS...mom

(a typewritten copy of this letter can be found in the Index page 124-125)

AFTERWORD

A month before he died, Chris told me he didn't want to grow up. Knowing what I know today, I would say to him, *I hope not.* As I look back, I am ashamed at how I reacted to him at times. As they say, hindsight is 20/20. It was his childlike spirit that made him the sensitive, caring, compassionate, charming man that he was. He wasn't immature. What appeared to be immaturity was his gift to all of us. It helped us to find our smile, our laughter and our hopes of being able to live in the moment with him. It was the only place that he could live. He had the gift.... of being able to find joy in the moment and turn it into laughter.

If Chris could sit on the top of Mt. Tam everyday of his life, he would. The question is a matter of belief and interpretation: Was he wasting away or was he actually bringing some meaning to our life as he would intimately and passionately share every bit of that experience with anyone who would take a moment to listen? Our spiritual teachers in life come in many forms. They are all around us at all times. Some refer to them as "the angels" that God sends to help us on this journey. Chris was one of mine. I bet if you are reading this and he was in your life; he was one of yours as well.

I've said to my clients many times over: We have to love **someone** deeply enough so we understand how to heal from a broken heart when and if we are "blessed" enough to have that experience. A line in one of Annie Lennox's songs from the 70s, says it well: "It's better to have loved and lost than never to have loved at all." But again it is a matter of belief and interpretation. Is our heart "breaking" or is it opening for a deeper awareness? These are choices we have to make. Remember, **<u>freewill</u>** comes with the freedom to choose where to go next with pain and suffering.

After my father passed away in 2000 I started to get pains in my chest. Since my father died of a heart attack, my PCP wanted me to immediately have a stress test. I knew that my heart was broken and when I said that to the staff monitoring the stress test, they were speechless. I had to find a way to live with the pain, and when I did, I was more prepared to handle the pain I would experience when my son died. Everything happens for a reason....

Thank you, Chris, for taking my hand and walking me through this journey to the bottom of my heart. I understand son why you asked ME to write this and I am truly humbled. As it is finally coming to its end for me, I hope that it can be the beginning of something grand for those of you who will read it. My son was so beautiful and he sincerely wanted you to have this for some reason. You are the only one who knows the reason. I hope it especially speaks to you, Jay, as he loved you more than anyone. Take his spirit with you, Jay, and he will show you how to live, laugh and love again.

My promise to you Chris is to continue to keep my heart open and love as deeply as I can.

SPECIAL THANKS

Special thanks goes out to Amanda Davis, who helped me get my mind organized to begin writing this manuscript when I would have my meltdowns. She was so generous with her time to edit this book. I was trapped in my mind and stuck in my heart a few times and she truly rescued me. Thank you so much sweetie.

I want to thank a dear friend, Kimmy Augustine, for her generosity and constant encouragement. All of those early morning text messages came at the right moment. You and Amanda are certainly my Earth angels.

Also a special thanks goes out to Jay, who put in a lot of time to format this book for publication. I know it was painful for you to keep reliving these memories. Thank you for helping me with the parts that I could not have done without you. I love you.

To all of my friends who tried to stay close to me while I was writing: I know I pushed you away and ignored your calls. It was so hard at times to keep my life balanced and I hope to get that back again. Thank you for being there for me. I have a place in my heart for all of you.

To my sister, Cookie, who listened to me cry and cried with me. She was patient enough every morning to take those early morning calls before I started my workday. She was always there for me as I needed to vent and needed someone to blow some air into my sails. Through good times and bad, you gave me your best and that's true for all of my family. I love you.

And to my little Pomeranian, Bella, who laid patiently with me during the evenings and weekends while I wrote. Spring is coming and we will get back to walking and playing in the yard. That is a promise! You are a bright spot in my life. You warm my heart.

Last but certainly not least, to my higher power that gives me the strength and courage to walk this path until it ends.

LOST NO MORE

Christopher Lee Burns

6/17/1983- 4/24/2007

......And may your spirit continue to shine as your soul rests in peace.

Index
Handwritten Letters to Me From My Son

Chris Burns

This year can be summed up as kind of a live, learn and move on kinda year. It started off the brand new year as a drastic and horrid thing which happened to me and my family. The leader of the family, the one in the family who made everyone laugh, always smiled, always helped out, especially was always there for anyone, and was very special and meant a lot to everyone, died. My grandpa died on New Years day of 2000, and it was the worst thing I ever had to go through. The call was around 8 in the morning and not only was I extremely hung over, but I was sick as well. My mom called over my friend's house which I was staying at and woke me up to hear...."grandpas dead, grandpas dead. It was hell. I completely went into shock and everything was slow motion from there. The drive home was so horrible. Once I went to his house there was a priest praying over him and I couldn't take it. I had to leave and go home and I just sat in my room staring and thinking for like 2 days, then I finally realized that everything happens for a reason, and death is inevitable, no one can stop it, and when it's time to go, it's time to go. I was able to get through my grandpas' death after the funeral and everything. I learned a lot from this experience. I learned that no one can stop death, what happens in life happens for a reason and no matter what happens one must move on from it and not grieve forever. All that can be done after a loved one is gone, is remember all the times that were shared, and just move on from it.

After this incident occurred, I almost died by getting nailed and totaled my car. I was thinking that this was going to be the worst year ever. Then after that incident, there was a clearing. I found a perfect girl for me who is nice, smart, beautiful, pleasant and everything I need in a girl. She's cool and I really like her a lot. After I met her it seems everything good happened. I pulled up my grades, I started lifting and got my size back, I got a job, and I'm just living life to the fullest. Some things happen in life that are unexpected and catch one off guard, but what ever happens just live, learn and move on.

Pg. 79-82

Ma,

Ya I can't believe I've succumbed this either. I am very disappointed in the way I've handled myself ever since day one that I've been down here in Florida. I am in aww that I've slipped back and regressed once again. As I sit in jail and think about everything, I think I am starting to second guess my motives of why I really wanted to come down here, which is a very scary thing. I knew I relapsed even before I was off probation. I couldn't understand why either. I have not been in the right mental state ever since I started using, which is totally my fault. I think the reason is that I am not ready to grow up and move on-I constantly think about the past and how great it was and how everything was perfect before

I started using. And night after night I'm up praying and desperately searching for an answer and some sort of reassurance that everything's going to be OK.

I've come to see that everything in my life and I was most happy when I was not using, and that is where I truly need to be again in my life. I am such a good kid w/the biggest heart you could ever imagine, but its just been steered in the wrong direction. I battle my addiction everyday of my life because I do not do what I am supposed to do-I just sit and wait for something, a miracle if you may, to just happen to me and make it all better-but now I've come to realize that finally I'm sick and tired of being sick and tired and the miracle needs to come from inside of me. And that is doing the right things, finally with my life. That means I have to give up and surrender-live a totally different life and totally change everything I've grown into the last 3 years. I need to reincarnate myself and really come to terms with what really matters in my life and the path I need to be on-I know you hear this from me a lot when I relapse, but I truly think this time I'm gonna get it. I've never felt like this before ever since I started using. Maybe the miracle did happen-jail. This place has enabled me to really sit and evaluate my life and let me see the future and consequences first-hand of where I was going. I've never been here and I think I needed this, plus it allowed me to become way more spiritual w/myself and God. Let me explain something to you-you said I don't realize the severity of the situation I am in-you know, your absolutely right. I have become so "numb" to disappointments in my life that at first, actually the first week I was in jail, I didn't even care-I did not even care. That is sick and degrading to me to think of the kid I once was, to what I am now that I do not even care that I am in JAIL?!!? How could I let my life slip like this and get to the point where I COULD CARE IF I WAS IN JAIL? I see a huge problem w/that, and the problem is me-my attitude and my outlook on life ever since I started using. I've come to a realization that everything in my life for the rest of my life is not going to be easy. I am ready to take this disease on first hand I think, for the first time since I started. Millions of people do it, so why can't I? I need to do the right thing with my life which means no drugs, no one from the past that uses, no more lying, attend meetings, gain a support group, get a non using girlfriend, become holier and surrender to God, pray and finally be the real Christopher Lee Burns that I once was. I was happiest when I wasn't using, and often the devil made his way to me, left his mark and now its time to grow up and end this non fruitful, terrible sinned life I've been living. And I think jail, and the consequences of being here led me to the path finally where I need to be on. All my struggles and downfalls have come with a price, but Mom please don't let that price ever be you giving up on me. You said your promise, well my promise to ME AND YOU will be from now on, I will never be the selfish asshole that would have to put you in the predicament to rescue me, ever again. I vouch that from this day on; I will find my way and be the person whom I truly am at heart, NOT this evil thing that I've turned into. I am so thankful, and everyday I pray and thank God that I have the family that I do, for my family is the absolutely only thing I have, and quite frankly I've come to learn that you guys are the only thing I need.

But from now on, I think I'm going to be ok, in fact what doesn't kill ya only makes you stronger and with that said I must be the strongest idiotic dumbass in all the land. But thank you mom for standing by me, because I promise you it'll only get better from this point on-everything will be OK

Love ya,

Chris

Pg. 113

Dear Chris,

June 17, 1983 was a day I'll never forget. How scared I was to go to the hospital because the doctors told me that there could possibly be something wrong with you...and the doctors were right, there was something different...**you were born an angel.** Tearfully, I counted every toe and finger...two eyes, a nose and strong arms and legs to carry you through life. Whew was I relieved! God knows, that those legs never stopped moving and that mouth never stopped talking! But **your smile**, Chris, it warmed every heart that saw it...especially mine.

I want to thank you for teaching me about life in ways that I could never have hoped or imagined. You taught me never to give up. Every time I watched you trying so hard to sound out words, write your name, and learn to ride your bike, or throw a ball...I knew that I would survive raising you and Jay! Only God knows how difficult that has been for me!

You taught me to see life through its differences...we know that not everyone is alike. You learned differently and so my life was different because of you. Your sensitivities, strength, courage and determination taught me that the challenges in life are not walls, but just bridges to get us exactly where we need to be. You showed me how to get there. I watched you do it. And therefore I could. And now, here you are, off to Mount Union ready to cross another bridge to get to where you want to be. How proud I am of you, Chris.

I watched you grow into the loving, caring, fun, attentive man that you are. You are a true inspiration for all men. When God gave you to me, I never realized the magnitude of the gift I would be given. Watching you grow has been such a joy for me...one of the most joyful experiences of my life.

It is time for you to move on and for me to remember everything that you have taught me...as I have to face my life alone after all of these years. Wherever you go in life, Chris, just know that there won't be a day in your life that I won't be thinking of you and praying that you will finally be living the life that you deserve. I can't thank you enough for being the "wind beneath my wings" on those days when I wasn't sure if I had the strength to keep on going... your warmth and smile always helped.

I hope that god will allow me to grow old with you because I can't imagine my life any other way. You are the most wonderful person I know in life...and how lucky I was that God picked me to be your mother. **That's how I know there is a God in my life...he sent me an angel, when he gave you to me.**

Thank you sweetheart, for all of the wonderful, tender memories that I will always carry in my heart. I am going to miss you more than you will ever know. I am your #1 fan ...so you go and make your life the BEST THAT IT CAN BE AND DON'T EVER EVER FORGET WHO YOU ARE....YOU ARE A BEAUTIFUL MAN... INSIDE...AND OUT.

I'LL LOVE YOU FOREVER AND ALWAYS....mom

If you or someone you love is struggling with drug addiction please contact:

National Intervention Referral at (800) 399-3612 for help

Other programs to consider:
TurnToHelpNow.com
www.journeyrecoverycenters.com
www.milestonesranch
www.nicd.us
naranoncafe.com
naranonforum.com
Alcoholics anonymous
Narcotics anonymous

If you have lost a child or know of someone who has the following programs can help with grief recovery

www.CompassionateFriends.org
www.CopeFoundation.org
LifeScript.com
Local.com

Photo credits and permission given for inserts:

**Pg. 10-11-permission given by Nancy
Layko for her email response**

**Pg. 30-permission given by Debbie Lenz
from Artistic Dermagraphics**

**Pg. 54-permission given to use this print from
Pamela Shane from Shane Photography**

Pg. 96-97-photo credit-Stephanie Golubic

Pg.98-photo credit-Jason Burns

**Pg. 99-100-permission by Todd Franko Editor of
the Youngstown Vindicator**

Pg. 106-108-permission given by Jason Burns

All other photo credits are from Jason Burns and the author

**To view additional pictures and information as a supplement
to this book, log on to www.lostnomore.us. The author can be
reached by logging onto lostnomore42407@yahoo.com**

CPSIA information can be obtained at www.ICGtesting.com
229770LV00005B/15/P